The Christian life is full of platitudes. One of these is that we "forgive one another." U _____ *quences of difficult a* _____ *Is it just "the way* _____ *that we all need u* _____ *will help you press* _____ *ituation. Run the r*

—Mi
    Pre
    Mc

"The bloc _____ *all who embrace t* _____ *can come together* _____ *the book When Y* _____ *tzer. Dr. Lutzer sk* _____ *Christians can have*

—F
    B
    S

Hardly _____ *broken promise* _____ *ristian homes* _____ *Lutzer urges us* _____ *d moving fror* _____ *ght and practica* _____ *to freedom an*

—Nancy Leigh DeMoss,
    Author, Revive Our Hearts radio host

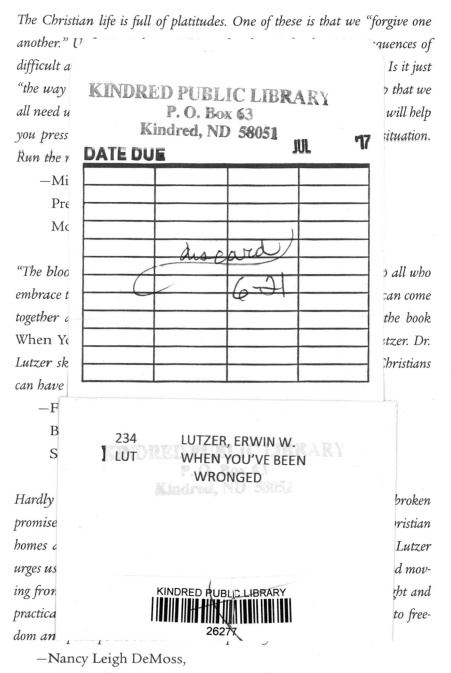

WHEN YOU'VE BEEN WRONGED

MOVING FROM BITTERNESS TO FORGIVENESS

ERWIN W. LUTZER

MOODY PUBLISHERS
CHICAGO

All Scripture quotations, unless otherwise indicated, are taken from the *Holy Bible, New International Version*®. NIV®. Copyright © 1973, 1978, 1984 by International Bible Society. Used by permission of Zondervan. All rights reserved.

Scripture quotations marked NKJV are taken from the *New King James Version.* Copyright © 1982 by Thomas Nelson, Inc. Used by permission. All rights reserved.

Scripture quotations marked THE MESSAGE are from *The Message,* copyright © by Eugene H. Peterson 1993, 1994, 1995. Used by permission of NavPress Publishing Group.

Cover Design: Kirk DuPonce / Dog Eared Design
Interior Design: Smartt Guys design
Editor: Jim Vincent

Library of Congress Cataloging-in-Publication Data

Lutzer, Erwin W.
    When you've been wronged : moving from bitterness to forgiveness /
by Erwin W. Lutzer.
        p. cm.
    ISBN-13: 978-0-8024-8897-8
    ISBN-10: 0-8024-8897-8
        1. Reconciliation—Religious aspects—Christianity. 2. Interpersonal conflict—Religious aspects—Christianity. 3. Forgiveness—Religious aspects—Christianity.
    I. Title.

BT738.27.L88 2007
234'.5—dc22

                                                                    2007009373

We hope you enjoy this book from Moody Publishers. Our goal is to provide high-quality, thought-provoking books and products that connect truth to your real needs and challenges. For more information on other books and products written and produced from a biblical perspective, go to www.moodypublishers.com or write to:

Moody Publishers
820 N. LaSalle Boulevard
Chicago, IL 60610

3 5 7 9 10 8 6 4 2

Printed in the United States of America

CONTENTS

INTRODUCTION:

THOSE IMPOSSIBLE PEOPLE

MANY CHRISTIANS ARE TRAPPED. Hurt by friends, relatives, and even members of the Christian community, they sit behind walls of animosity and deep-seated anger. The Devil, ever seeking an advantage in his war against God's people, has many of them immobilized, waiting for the elusive day when the wrongs will be made right and they will be vindicated. Until then, they are not interested in reconciliation and forgiveness.

Many have taken themselves out of the race of life to mark time, waiting for a day of exoneration. Indeed, reconciliation with those who have hurt us—or those whom we have hurt— sometimes appears impossible.

And so you sit. Or perhaps you watch others sit. We've all met people whose careful and repeated nursing of wrongs has so embittered them that they are not only unwilling to forgive, but their expectations of what others should do for them are so unreasonable that they are condemned to live without the benefit of restored friendships.

In the face of overwhelming evidence, some refuse to admit that they have done wrong and as a price of reconciliation, they expect the other person to admit to things of which the other person is innocent. Others desire reconciliation only as a further excuse to control those from whom they are estranged. Former friends, acquaintances, and family must become subject to their notions about what others owe them and perceived injustices that must be made right. These people are destroyers, whom we shall meet in later chapters of this book.

Jesus knew that we as humans would hurt each other, either intentionally or unintentionally. He knew that some people would lead others astray either because of false doctrine or a false view of life itself. Jesus was saying, in effect, that it is inevitable that some people will offend others. In Matthew 18:7 He warned, "Woe to the world because of the things that cause people to sin! Such [offenses] must come, but woe to the man through whom they come!"

TAKING OFFENSE

That word "offense" is actually the Greek word *scandalon*, from which we get our English words "scandal" or "scandalized." Originally, the word was used to refer to the bait used to snare a wild animal. It can be translated as "snare" or "an offense," and refers to anything that hinders our walk with God.

This is the word that is used in Matthew 16:23, when Peter,

out of affection for his Master, attempted to prevent Him from going to the cross. Jesus rebuked Peter saying, "Get behind me, Satan! You are a stumbling block [*scandalon*] to me; you do not have in mind the things of God, but the things of men."

Jesus did not fall into Peter's trap, but sometimes we fall into the Devil's trap of bitterness or a misperception of ourselves that we justify with compelling arguments and repeated pronouncements of personal innocence. Yet, offenses we refuse to give up not only injure us emotionally, but they have the potential to exact an enormous spiritual toll. If not put behind us, they can have eternal repercussions.

Consider the other side of the coin: For every person wronged, there is someone who has done the wrong. What this means is that many—perhaps about half—who are reading this introduction see themselves as victims of injustice, but in point of fact, they have also perpetrated injustice and cruelty of various kinds! As we will discover, we are usually blind to our own faults, magnifying the failure of others and minimizing our own.

So this book is written to both groups—the people who believe they have been wronged and the people who have done the wrong but protest their innocence. God has a word to both the hurt and the "hurters," that is, those who inflict pain on others but are deeply convinced about the rightness of their cause.

HEARING WHAT GOD IS SAYING

As you read this book, hear these words not just as applying to others, but listen to what God is saying to you. Unless we see our own failures, we will never be able to deal fairly and biblically with the failures of others. Unless we are willing to be honest about our own sins, we will always distort and overreact to the sins of others. Thankfully, the Holy Spirit is with us to reveal our own needy hearts.

Marriages are broken, churches are split, and believers are stalled in their tracks spiritually because they have not properly responded to offenses. They've become bitter and defensive, critical and hard-hearted, and Satan uses the offense to keep them bound. There is a wall between them and God that they do not want removed.

We remember offenses better and longer than we do the good deeds that others have done for us. Ask someone what they remember about their early school days and they will probably refer to an offense: "I remember when I was humiliated in the seventh grade." We forget the good times; we remember the wrongs done to us.

How long will it take you to forget that a friend never paid you back for money you loaned to him? Especially when you know he has the money because he bought a new car! Will you forget about it in five years, or ten? Fact is, we carry these kinds of offenses to the grave.

Or perhaps a friend broke a confidence; you have felt betrayed. I know someone with whom I shared information and he agreed to keep it in confidence, but later I learned he told others. I felt betrayed, and to this day I think of the incident when I meet him. Years ago I put this offense behind me, but the truth is I wouldn't trust him with confidential matters again.

How long does it take a young woman to forget the boyfriend who promised his undying love, but after getting the sensual relationship he wanted, he discarded her like the peelings of an orange? The lies, the betrayal, the feeling of being used, sticks like Velcro in her heart. The memories are taken to the grave, and unfortunately it is also possible that the consequences of those memories will mar her entire life.

"One cutting, bitter word given in the summer," someone has said, "can last all winter!" In fact, it can last for many winters to come. Recently, I spoke to a pastor who was betrayed by his church board. They caved in to the evil schemes of a control freak and refused to discipline the man who brought outlandish accusations against this man of God. This minister's wound is still open, too fresh for a Band-Aid. He doesn't know if he can trust anyone. As the saying goes, "If you've been burned on skim milk, you will even blow on yogurt!"

Yes, time is needed to heal such wounds, but how much time? Some people keep their wound as fresh as it was the day the knife was thrust into their heart. For them, time does not heal because the offense is carefully nourished, kept fresh by the mind's tape recorder that is often switched on involuntarily.

Offenses and the collateral damage they cause can be powerful instruments of Satan. Such offenses can debilitate you and keep you struggling and render you ineffective as a believer. Knowing how Satan uses offenses by building up walls between you and God or you and others is the first step in moving ahead spiritually and getting unstuck from your past.

No two stumbling blocks are alike. A friend of mine relayed a tragic tale of a young man who many years ago attended a mission conference at Moody Church where I serve. He and a friend sat spellbound, clearly under the conviction of the Holy Spirit, as they listened to the evening speaker. He spoke passionately on the Great Commission and ended his message with a call for young people to surrender to full-time Christian service. The young visitor, so under the Spirit's conviction, turned to his friend, a Moody student, and said, "I believe the Lord is calling me into missions. I want to be a missionary pilot. Will you go forward with me?" They both responded and made their way to the front of the sanctuary where the young man prayed a prayer of total surrender.

When he returned home and told his parents of his decision, they laughed at him. They then proceeded to threaten to disinherit him if he followed through with such a ridiculous notion! His spirit wilted at their response. He never spoke again about that night at Moody Church. His parents and their words had become to him an *offense*—a *scandalon* that caused him to stumble from God's best.

Can such an offense be overcome? Can that injury be healed and a life be restored? The answer is *yes*. But only through the grace and forgiveness of Christ can anyone find lasting deliverance and healing from the binding power of an offense. My prayer is that this book will lay a path for you.

A PATH TO FOLLOW

This is a book about offenses; it is a book about both success and failure in reconciliation. Above all, it is a book designed to help us clear our conscience and experience freedom in our relationship with God. It is a book to enable us to move beyond what others have done to us, looking to the future and not the past. It is a book about boundaries that need to be in place to limit the influence of toxic people who desire that their poison be spread to as many of us as possible.

No matter the cost, our conscience must be cleared so that we are rid of the nagging feeling that part of our past has been left undone. A clear conscience allows you to live your life free of offense—before God and before others. To be candid: I believe genuine reconciliation to be the stuff of revival; because once our souls are unclogged of bitterness and hurt, the Spirit of God has freedom to move and heal. The body of Christ today includes countless bitter, hurting, and wounded people—bound by the power of a personal offense. Yet where the Spirit of the Lord is there is liberty—and liberty brings revival.

When these messages were preached at Moody Church, hundreds of people responded, determined that they would no longer carry the offenses that had hindered their walk with God. In letting God free them, they discovered they could free others so that the name of Christ is honored in our churches and families.

May the following pages open a path toward healing and personal revival. Let's walk the path together with God's help.

CHAPTER 1

SATAN'S MIXED BAG OF OFFENSES

"WHAT YOU DON'T FORGIVE, you pass on" a counselor wisely pointed out to a woman whose husband lived a double life for twenty-five years. Only when he was dying of AIDS did she realize that the man she had tried so hard to trust had deceived her and potentially could have passed the disease on to her. Now, a few years after his demise, she was faced with a decision: Should she keep her anger and desire for vengeance alive, or would she give it up for her own benefit and in obedience to the Lord she had come to love?

In this chapter we will describe some of the common offenses that many of us have had to bear, and in the next chapter we will describe what happens to those who do not deal with offenses in healthy ways. If you have never been offended, or if you are not facing a difficult standoff with another person, you can still benefit from this chapter by grasping the dilemma of some who feel keenly the pain of broken relationships.

BETRAYAL

King David, the second king of Israel, was no stranger to personal offenses. Not only was he a hurter at times, inflicting his own brand of justice on the unsuspecting, he himself endured occasions when enemies railed against him because of his trust in God. But the most painful times in David's life were those when people closest to him betrayed him. Few things are more painful to us than when someone close to us wounds us deeply.

Read carefully David's words in Psalm 55. Perhaps you can relate to the intensity of his struggle.

> Listen to my prayer, O God, do not ignore my plea; hear me and answer me. My thoughts trouble me and I am distraught at the voice of the enemy, at the stares of the wicked; for they bring down suffering upon me and revile me in their anger. My heart is in anguish within me. (Psalm 55:1–4)

Clearly, the offense David described brought him to the point of anguish and despair. But it's not until later in the psalm that he reveals the surprising source of the injury—a personal friend.

If an enemy were insulting me, I could endure it; if a foe were raising himself against me, I could hide from him. But it is you, a man like myself, my companion, my close friend, with whom I once enjoyed sweet fellowship as we walked with the throng at the house of God. (verses 12–14)

David admits that such offenses would be a little easier to endure coming from his enemies—he'd expect that from them. But he puts powerful expression to those difficult feelings we've all felt when we've been injured by a close friend or a loved one or someone we believed we could trust.

That's one of the reasons why divorces grow nasty and bitter. It's because someone I love, someone who is in my house, someone with whom I shared a bed has become my vilest enemy. It happens among business partners and ministry colleagues as well. And because so much rides on these personal relationships, Satan loves to inflict his harm. Often these offenses seem amazingly petty and inconsequential—but in the hands of the Enemy they can exact inestimable damage.

WHAT'S IN THE BAG?

Satan uses a mixed bag of offenses to keep people bound. Let's examine a few of them, and then in the next chapter we will find out what happens to these unresolved issues within the human heart. This will help us understand why reconciliation is often so difficult and sometimes impossible.

The first painful offense in this bag is a *broken promise*. Hear the cry of this woman: "Pray for me again . . . I failed the human test. I believed another man's lies that he was going to marry me. Of course I broke God's Word's teaching about sex. I am a Christian woman and love Jesus with all my heart. But I'm weak when it comes to the human touch. Men continue to lie and I believe them. . . . I am so deceived and Satan uses this need of mine."

Her letter goes on to say that she dated the man for two years, they served in a church together, and he appeared to be everything she had prayed for. But when his parents discovered that the two wanted to get married, they turned on their son, fearing they were losing control over him. They said that his girlfriend had no right to expect marriage, particularly because she was not properly meeting his sexual needs anyway. He in turn began having sex with a woman he met on the Internet, and now he cursed the woman he had promised to marry. The depth of her anger can be felt as she continues: "I had no idea I was dating a demon controlled by 'devil parents.'"

This dear woman—may God help her—says she has been abused by men since she was fourteen, and she is now forty-six years old. This man was one of a long list of men who had deceived her, and he chose to break their relationship on her birthday to add insult to injury. What this woman does with her pain is very important and will determine her mental health in the years to come.

To a lesser degree, all of us have experienced the pain of betrayal. You lend a friend money and he says, "You know I'll get it back to you as soon as I have it." Later on, he has a job and prospers and when he sees you he pretends as if everything is fine.

I heard of a dentist who did a lot of work for Christians. He stopped going to church because he said there were too many choir members singing through teeth he had fixed that had not been paid for! Broken promises actually caused him to renounce church! A broken leg may heal so well that the event is long forgotten; broken promises can cause lifelong injury.

A young pastor began a ministry on Saturday mornings to the inmates of the local county jail. Each week he'd go into the jail cells and conduct Bible studies and prayer sessions among the inmates—mostly young white men who were doing time for anything from burglary to habitual drug use. As he'd enter the jail the despair and anger among these nineteen- to twenty-four-year-olds was palpable. When the young pastor asked the warden how so many young men with great promise could end up in such a place, the warden sighed and said, "This place is filled with boys who got tired of waiting for their dads to keep their promises—promises to provide, promises to show up and spend time with them, promises to come home at night—they finally got so angry with the injustice of it, they went out and did stupid things."

Young men waiting for their dads to keep their promises! What a sobering reminder that broken promises can help send a young man down a road of personal destruction. Accept the fact that all of us live with promises we have broken or promises others have made to us that were not kept.

The second offense in this bag is the *breaking of confidence*.

A young man told his pastor about his struggle with homosexuality. He thought that his frank talk was confidential, since he was earnestly seeking help. Yet, a few weeks later, the pastor blurted out in a sermon, "Recently a young man in our church shared his own struggles with homosexual tendencies. . . ." He gave enough other details for people in the small congregation to suspect that it was the young man who had indeed shared his inmost thoughts and battles. Rumors began circulating and the crushed young man left the church never to return again. Humiliated, betrayed, used.

Where do you turn when people you thought you could trust betray your inner soul? Sadly, many churches have split, friendships ended, and ministries struggled amid the turbulence of breached confidences.

Satan's bag contains a third offense: *personal rejection*. We could include in this category all sorts of verbal, emotional, and racial rejection as well as slander and gossip. I recall as a boy learning that ditty, "Sticks and stones will break my bones, but names will never harm me." I don't know who wrote it, but it should be banned! Who hasn't felt the sting of an unkind word, or a teasing remark from a bully or peer, or from a racial slur? Such barbs slice deep into the human soul. One cutting remark has the power to paralyze a child's emotional development and send him/her to a life of compensating for the hurt.

Fourth, this bag contains the offense of a *false accusation*. For instance, a teenage girl, motivated by jealousy, falsely accuses a boy of something he didn't do. When he denies it, the two families wind up in a feud over the truth. The offenses shatter all trust and the relationships become strained and hollow. And at times, the rupture from a false accusation can run so deep that reconciliation seems impossible. Walls go up so high they become virtually impenetrable.

A BAGFUL OF PAIN

The offense—and sometimes offenses—that can bring pain into your life and relationships are engineered by Satan to attempt to bind you and me to sin. The offenses are:

1. *A broken promise.* Do you still remember a broken promise? Have you forgiven the person who broke it?
2. *A broken confidence.* If someone has betrayed your confidence, how have you responded?
3. *Personal rejection.* This includes not only verbal and emotional rejection but slander and gossip as well.
4. *False accusation.* Being charged falsely with wrongdoing can hurt your reputation and damage relationships. It is difficult to forgive the accuser and restore trust.
5. *Abuse.* Physical or verbal abuse often leaves enduring emotional scars. God, however, can bring healing and the ability to forgive the abuser.

Fifth, this bag holds the awful offense of *abuse,* such as when the parent inflicts physical and emotional pain upon a child. These hurts penetrate into the life and perception of a child who will struggle with anger and self-hatred, and this baggage will be taken with him into adulthood. At first glance it seems as if there can be no redeemable value to the evil that is being inflicted upon some children even as you read this paragraph. The horrors are too gruesome to describe, and the emotional wounds are difficult to turn into scars that would prove that healing has taken place. Yet, even here we must believe in God's grace and healing.

Five ugly pieces of pain. Any one or more of these offenses results in a broken relationship, and typically the offended becomes enflamed with bitterness and resentment. Satan exploits the pain by making it the central focus of the man's (or woman's) thoughts and attitudes. The Enemy jumps at the chance to debilitate a potentially effective follower of Christ by using a personal offense to hold him or her in spiritual limbo.

BARRIERS TO RECONCILIATION

Two sisters had grown apart throughout the years, the younger one rejecting a Christian lifestyle and the older one following Christ wholeheartedly. The younger, Christine, who married unhappily, evidently resented her older sister who is married to a fine Christian man. Despite their differences in outlook and values, Christine frequently calls Monica, wanting to "get together."

But the conversation typically goes something like this . . .

"You never come to see us."

"We want to, Christine, but when we do you always find some reason to not be available."

"Well, there are lots of reasons. Our children are all over the house . . . You know, it's hard to keep the place clean. Anyway, you haven't exactly been supporting me over the years. I mean, why didn't you defend me when Mom and Dad were abusing me?"

"I was only a girl of nine at the time and there wasn't much I could do because at that time I didn't realize how serious it all was."

"When I was sleeping with Don before we were married, you didn't support me either."

"Well, no, I believed it was wrong then and I believe it is wrong now."

"Yeah, but that shows you hate me, don't you?"

"No, I don't hate you. . . . I have never hated you."

"Sure you hate me. Come on, Monica! You never defended me when Mom and Dad were abusing me and you refused to support my marriage. Ever since Don and I slept together, you've thought you were better than me.

"And I resent that Mom and Dad gave you money for college but they didn't give any to me."

"I didn't ask Mom and Dad for money for college."

"Well, maybe not, but you took it and you didn't care about me."

"I did care about you, I—"

"You hate me and you've always taken advantage of me."

"No, I don't hate you, Christine, and we will try to visit, but we have to agree on some rules between your children and mine."

"So that's what you think of me! You think my children aren't good enough for your goody-two-shoes kids!! You think your kids are perfect, right? You believe they are perfect and my kids are devils. That's what you think, isn't it?"

"No, that's not what I think . . . I just know that when the kids get together, yours are a little wild . . . uh, they need guidance. I mean, we just have to agree on some things for our family to visit you."

"See, you do hate me . . . and you think I'm evil, don't you?"

Monica feels as though she's been slapped in the face. Her eyes begin to water. She wonders, *Have I just accused my sister?*

"Chris, you are *not evil*, and I have never hated you. But I must admit that you have eroded some trust by the lies you've told me in the past."

"So, since you claim to be a Christian, then where is your forgiveness? I can't believe the way you hold grudges, bringing up things that go back a couple of years—and *you still remember those things! What a memory!*"

Enough.

Do you think there is any chance that these two sisters can get together for a nice leisurely stroll in the park? I don't think so . . .

In the next chapter we will discover why the bitter Christine puts up barriers to reconciliation that Monica finds impossible to overcome. We'll discover the blinding power of bitterness, the blinding power of an offense.

And in the process, we might just discover ourselves.

A PRAYER FOR HONESTY

Father, I pray that You will give me the honesty to let You uncover the hidden sins I've tolerated because of my past. Help me look at all that happened, and then spill my bitterness like a pitcher of water at the foot of Jesus' cross. Deliver me from the irrationality of sin, which makes me defensive and suspicious of all relationships. Let my words to others be wholesome, wise, and true. In Jesus' name. Amen.

CHAPTER 2

THE BLINDING POWER OF AN OFFENSE

WHEN AN OFFENSE FESTERS in our hearts, we cannot confine it within our souls. Instead, it spills over in ways that we don't even realize. It's like burning incense in a dormitory. The smell cannot be confined; rather it escapes the dorm room and wafts down the hallway, into the washrooms, and all the way to the front door. Just so, our bitterness spills over into other relationships no matter how determined we are to keep it confined to a single room within our soul. Nursing an offense quite literally blinds us to our own faults, forces us to have skewed relationships, and warps our self-perceptions.

This chapter outlines five characteristics of someone who is in bondage to an offense. Some who nurture their offense have almost all of these characteristics; some might only have one or two. The nature of the offense determines the kind of response we might have. In general, I believe these character traits are an accurate and biblical picture of a person focused on their inner pain.

1. WALLED IN BY BITTERNESS

Meet a bitter person and you will find someone with thick walls designed to protect his or her own resentment. These walls of internalized anger and mistrust have deep foundations that support a well-insulated fortress mentality. Solomon described this reality in Proverbs 18:19: "An offended brother is more unyielding than a fortified city, and disputes are like the barred gates of a citadel."

Solomon says you can more easily conquer a castle than reconcile an offended brother or friend. Just as you can't remove the barred gates of a castle, you sometimes cannot peaceably enter the life of a wounded brother or sister. Scaling a stone wall is one thing; winning over a stony heart is another.

A few years ago my wife and I visited Rotenburg, Germany —a medieval city whose fortress walls remain standing to this day. In fact, we were able to walk on top of a good portion of those ancient walls. We also took a midnight tour with a guide who played the part of a medieval watchman.

We already knew that the reason walls were built around a city was to control what would be allowed into the city. But our tour guide actually showed us the small manhole which at night was all that remained open, just big enough for one person to crawl through. If you arrived after the gates were locked you were allowed passage through this small opening, only after personal identification, assuring the guards you did not pose a threat to the city. Everyone who came through was carefully inspected.

That's precisely how injured people operate. An offended brother builds high walls to make certain no enemy combatant penetrates his life again. Only information or people that affirm his pain are allowed into the fortress of his life. The manhole is carefully monitored, making sure that no one will challenge his right to deep bitterness and resentment. The pain is too great to allow someone to get very close and risk another attack.

In other words, all information that is favorable to him is allowed entry and encouraged; information that will challenge or admonish him will be filtered out. He will spend time with friends who can be trusted to confirm his bitterness, to help justify his feelings. He will dare anyone to suggest that he bears some responsibility, even in those instances where it is obvious to others that he does. Meanwhile, those who would suggest that he was also responsible, or that he must forgive, are evicted from the premises of his mind and heart.

Even the most gracious and calculated argument will meet an impregnable defense. Facts are skewed, information is twisted, and sometimes reality is ignored in order to justify bitterness and anger. The offense becomes the all-encompassing center of his life and motivation.

2. BLIND TO PERSONAL FAULTS

John the apostle wrote these astounding words, "But whoever hates his brother is in the darkness and walks around in the darkness; he does not know where he is going, because the darkness has blinded him" (1 John 2:11). When you walk in darkness you are blind to your personal faults. Since only those who agree with your pain are allowed an entrance into your soul, you choose a path where you are able to see the wrongdoings of others with undimmed clarity, but you will be near stone-blind to your own glaring faults.

Jesus spoke about such blind spots when teaching about judging others:

> Why do you look at the speck of sawdust in your brother's eye and pay no attention to the plank in your own eye? How can you say to your brother, "Let me take the speck out of your eye," when all the time there is a plank in your own eye? (Matthew 7:3–4)

In these words, Jesus humorously describes the person who thinks he has a speck of dust in his own eye but sees a beam in the eye of a friend. But in reality, Jesus says, the opposite is true: The judgmental person actually has a beam in his own eye and what he sees in others is but a speck. Indeed, he only *thinks* he sees a beam in his friend's eye not knowing that *the supposed beam in his brother's eye is but a reflection of the beam which is in his own eye.* In fact, his beam is so big it has blinded him so that he cannot see others objectively. He has a willing blindness that gives him permission to deny his own faults.

Emotionally injured people are typically extremely judgmental toward others. They manage their pain by magnifying the faults of others and minimizing their own. They don't understand that the anger others have provoked in them is the same anger they are now provoking in others. Satan has used their pain to blind them to the hurt they inflict on those around them. As a result, wounded people often justify wounding others as retaliation for their injury. They never find the healing they need because they are not looking for it; they have another agenda and that is to take out their hurt on others, and they do so with both conscious and unconscious tactics.

What the bitter, offended person is saying is this: "My hurt is so deep, the offense done to me is so great that nothing I do can be as bad as what has been done to me." So he therefore believes he has the right to hurt others. All hope of seeing himself for what he is, has vanished. He denies his bitterness when he can and justifies it when it is pointed out. To forgive, he believes, would be to trivialize the offense, so the wound is carefully nurtured and kept fresh day after day.

In essence, sin deceives him. Author Steve Gallagher describes sin's hidden deception:

> People are prone to overlook their deeply embedded sin because it has an extremely deceptive nature. There exists an interesting correlation between a person's involvement with sin and his awareness of it. The more a person becomes involved in sin, the less he sees it. Sin is a hideous disease that destroys a person's ability to comprehend its existence. It could be compared to a computer virus that has the ability to hide its presence from the user while it systematically destroys the hard drive. Typically, those who are the most entangled in

sin are the very ones who cannot see its presence at work inside them. Sin has the ability to mask itself so well that it can actually make a person who deals with it the least, think he is the most spiritual.[1]

No wonder Paul warned that we should not be deceived by the "deceitfulness of sin"! Gallagher says *the person who refuses to deal with his sin often thinks he is the most spiritual!*

3. IN SEARCH OF VENGEANCE

Look carefully at bitterness and you will find pride and a desire for vengeance. Paul urged the believers in Rome to guard against being deceived in their arrogance. He wrote,

> Bless those who persecute you; bless and do not curse. Rejoice with those who rejoice; mourn with those who mourn. Live in harmony with one another. Do not be proud, but be willing to associate with people of low position. Do not be conceited. (Romans 12:14–16)

Our wounded pride and desire for revenge gets in the way of being rightly related to God and others. Paul went on to urge these people not to "repay anyone evil for evil." But to "be careful to do what is right in the eyes of everybody" (verse 17). Often a person who holds an offense takes matters into his own hands and retaliates. Vengeance, in his mind, is identified with justice. But Frances Beacon rightly called vengeance "wild justice."

It is easy to become obsessive/compulsive with a burning

desire that the offender pay for his offenses. We want him/her to pay every farthing with compound interest. Grace and forgiveness are seen to be impossibly unfair and unjust; only vengeance will do. "What would you like to see happen to your husband?" I asked a woman who had been grossly betrayed by the man who had sworn to love her till death did them part. "Hell will do," she said.

When I take vengeance into my hands I am doing God's work for Him; I cannot trust God to do what needs to be done, so I will do it. A vengeful person is one who is not broken before God (in the best sense of the term) but still insists on the control of his own life. He refuses to see God in his pain, and so he believes the matter must be taken up by himself. This is why Paul wrote, "Do not take [your own] revenge, my friends, but leave room for God's [revenge]" (Romans 12:19).

Since the bitter person refuses to loosen his bitter resolve, he obsesses over trying to convince God and everyone else to hate the people whom he hates. That kind of prideful resentment holds him in bondage. If he were told that he is actually aiding and abetting the Devil in his desire for vengeance, he would be offended. He believes he is doing the work of God; after all, God is on the side of justice and rightness, which is where he sees himself firmly planted.

Have you ever heard someone to be fired from a job say, "I got what was coming; they did the right thing!" No, almost always there is defensiveness, complaints about unfairness, and the desire to set the record straight. So the employee will go to his friends and recruit others to agree with him, and join him in his silent (or not so silent) protest. Usually, the matter ends with a hope that God will heap vengeance on those who treated him so "cruelly."

I had a friend who felt people wronged him at the Christian organization where he worked. They had made promises they

ARE YOU IN BONDAGE?

Those who have been offended and nurture the offense typically exhibit one or more of the following traits. Look at these and ask whether you are in bondage to any of them:

1. *Walled in by bitterness.* Bitter feelings can form thick walls designed to protect our own resentment.
2. *Blind to personal faults.* We may choose to see the wrongdoings of others with undimmed clarity, even as we become blind to our own glaring faults.
3. *In search of vengeance.* Our wounded pride can lead to a desire for revenge. We want the offender to pay for his offenses. But if we enact vengeance, we are doing what should be God's work alone (see Romans 12:19).
4. *Bent on destruction.* In the quest for vengeance, we can become destroyers, using manipulation, threats, accusations, discord, or other tactics in an attempt to destroy the one who has offended us.
5. *Given to idolatry.* We may make the offense into an idol of utmost importance. In effect, painful resentment and bitterness can replace our affection and devotion to God.

had not kept, he said, and he felt they treated him with condescending aloofness. He truly believed he was right and they were terribly wrong. When he was let go, anger welled up inside of him, and his pride prompted him to pray vengefully that God would shut the place down.

Years later he confessed that all God had done since he left was to bless the ministry! The work flourished and God used it mightily in the lives of countless people. Those folks who believe that if they left the church or an organization it would collapse, they need to know that God does not share our narrow, self-aggrandizing appraisal.

Haven't we all, at times, noticed that God blesses some people whom we think He shouldn't bless?! Who of us has not had to stand by while God bestows many different honors on someone whom we think should receive the opposite? Thankfully, God does bless those who don't deserve it, or else not one of us would receive His blessings!

Pride gives us a wrong perspective. God, in His wisdom, sees things differently. That's what our pride does—it deceives us, especially when we've suffered a wrong.

When my wife and I were at Ground Zero, the center of the September 2001 terrorist attacks on the World Trade Center in New York City, we watched a woman walk back and forth and up and down the street, shouting repeatedly, "Bush and the CIA did what you see here!"

I had two thoughts: First, I thought, *Isn't it wonderful that in America all kinds of people can give their viewpoint, even those who have a lively imagination?* Second, I marveled at the power of lingering hatred. When you hate a person you will attribute to him the basest of motives; you will filter out anything you hear about him that is good and embellish all that is bad. When the good your enemy has done cannot be denied, it will be re-interpreted as a cover for further evil. All that matters to the hateful heart is latching onto something that confirms your hatred and affirms your pain. There is no need for facts; no need for perspective, no need for objectivity. Hate makes you vulnerable to lies you are anxious to believe.

Keep in mind that people like this are thoroughly con-vinced about the rightness of their viewpoint! Those relatives who treat you like dirt—the ones who go out of their way to make life miserable for you—they believe you have it coming! They are convinced that any pain they can inflict on you is more than justified; indeed, if they were perfectly just, they'd even treat you a lot worse! Be thankful!

Offenses have the power to blind, to distort, and to spin reality in a new, warped direction.

4. BENT ON DESTRUCTION

A person offended can very quickly become what the Bible calls a destroyer, the same description that is given to the Devil who opposes all that heals and blesses. If you told someone who is in the process of destroying someone else that he/she is in league with the Devil, they would be incredulous. They do not see themselves as doing the work of the Devil but as doing the work of God—or at least the work that God *should* be doing.

Destroyers have many arsenals in their weaponry. Some do their damage by manipulation, others sow discord. Many love to pick fights or to destabilize others with threats or false accusations. When you speak to them they will take everything that is said and twist it a half turn. Like a blotter, they soak up everything but get it backwards.

Any one of us can become a destroyer. In warning of the tactics of Satan, Jesus said, "The thief comes only to steal and kill and destroy; I have come that they may have life" (John 10:10). An offended person who never heals can become like the Devil, bent on irrational, vengeful destruction.

Keep in mind that there are some people who get their sense of significance from destroying others. As a pastor I've had a front row seat to some of the most vicious attacks *by* God's people *on* God's people—all because of the binding power of an offense. There are people whose entire sense of value, and self-worth, and power is tied up in their desire to lord it over others and punish them for their misdeeds. It's often seen in families—between in-laws and relatives. In every case, relationships are destroyed and lasting wounds inflicted.

Beware, because destroyers can be charmers who appear devoted to their families and to God. Some men who abuse their families are so well thought of at church that other women wish they were married to them—after all, they are so kind and helpful. Yet, at home they are monsters—demanding, irrational, and angry. And they are completely convinced that they are right and all who disagree with them are wrong.

Ever wonder why so many divorces become messy and just plain evil? The husband might have paid very little attention to the children when the family was together, but now that he and his wife are about to separate, he fights for custody. He wants to prove that he is a caring father and most important, he wants to hurt his wife as deeply as he can. This is his chance to "get even," to "sock it to her" and make sure she gets what she deserves. He will destroy her if necessary to get what he wants, all to prove that he is a caring father.

I often tell the story about the man who walks into a bar where some drunken friend smears some smelling, rotten cheese onto his buddy's mustache. As he walks out into the night and breathes in the clear air, he groans to himself, "The whole world stinks." Have you met people like that? They are bitter and the whole world around them knows it. They're miserable and they want everyone around them to share their misery. The prospects for such people ever enjoying a meaningful and healthy relationship are bleak. But with God all things are possible.

5. GIVEN TO IDOLATRY

This might be the most startling characteristic of all: A person who will not get beyond his bitterness is actually an idolater. Let me clarify what I mean by asking this question: What would it take for you to turn away from God? If God took your children or spouse would you leave God? What if you were in a debilitating accident or if you discovered you had a fatal disease?

Or—think about this—might you turn away from God because the Almighty does not set the record straight about the wrongs done to you? Could it be that insisting on immediate justice for an offense means more to you than fellowship with God? Think of the young people who have said of their Christian parents, "Because I hate them, I also hate their God!"

When I was in high school I knew a student who was

involved in an accident. Though he recovered well, he was scarred in such a way that he became the object of ridicule by my friends and me. This was a Christian high school, and we all should have known better. But we were mean, like so many kids today. Besides that, he laughed along with us. We didn't think we were hurting him too much. Eventually, we all graduated and went our separate ways.

About ten years ago a mutual friend wrote to me and said that this man had left the church and turned his back on God. He traced his rejection of God all the way back to the pain we had caused him by making fun of his scars. I felt instant regret. I wrote the man a letter and begged for his forgiveness. I said that what we had done was unchristian and inexcusable, and that I longed for his undeserved forgiveness. To this day I've not heard a word of reply. Apparently, the pain we inflicted had been lifelong.

But here's the point: Believe it or not, that man actually kept this offense as an idol. He had allowed that painful resentment and bitterness to replace his affection and devotion to God. In effect he said, "I'm willing to give up on God until this other matter is resolved. And unless I get vengeance, I can tell God to 'take a hike.'"

Clearly, his relationship with God is optional; his need for immediate vengeance is not. Thus, his bitterness, like ours, can become an obsessive idol of the heart. When John wrote, "Dear children, keep yourselves from idols" (1 John 5:21), he probably was not referring to idols of stone, but the idols we set up in our hearts. Even a toxic emotion can become an object of idolatry.

Years ago I had a scab that I liked to itch; in fact itching it gave me a great feeling. My fingernails would always keep the wound open. No matter how good it felt, it would have been better for me to stop itching it and let the wound turn into a scar, proof that healing had taken place.

Talk to some offended people and they will spill out their resentment to anyone who is willing to listen. You'd think that the offense happened yesterday, last month, or last year. Turns out it happened twenty years ago, but the wound is constantly opened, constantly talked about, or constantly used as an excuse for one thing or another.

In Bible college I had a close and gifted friend who was deeply offended because of what he perceived was the lack of piety on the part of some of us. He did not believe that Christians should tell jokes, pull pranks, or even play sports. He was indeed serious-minded, sobered by the realities of the gospel and the need to "keep the faith." He refused to return for his final year, abandoning the faith and pursuing the world, convinced that our lightheartedness was proof enough that the Christian faith was but a shimmering mirage.

I'm not justifying myself or my other friends in Bible college; God knows, we might have been too impious. But what this young man was saying was, "My relationship with God is derailed because my friends have offended God and I am offended along with him." I've often wondered how Jesus will deal with this gifted young preacher at the judgment seat of Christ. Will He say, "You had good reason to leave the faith, because those students were out of line!"? I suspect Jesus will not accept his excuse but strongly rebuke him.

Do you see how easily you can give up on God and put your relationship with Him on hold? That's idolatry, plain and simple. And the Devil can keep you bound, paralyzed in your Christian walk. How easy it is to fall into his trap.

WHERE TO GO FROM HERE

Perhaps you've come to the end of this chapter and realized that you are in bondage to an offense. You need God's healing. You've tried to let go. You've tried to bury the pain and bitterness. You've realized how selfishly and arrogantly you've hung onto your pain and now it has become your idol. Your only path to healing is the path of surrender.

First, you must confront your idols of bitterness. What offense is standing between you and your relationship with God? Is there something that somebody did or some offense that cleaves to your soul? Often we can't see those idols unless God reveals them to us. So you need some time in God's presence to allow Him to show you your idol. Don't think you can do this hurriedly; it takes time to be holy.

Second, you must turn the offense—the stumbling block —into a stepping-stone to growth. God is saying, "If you can overcome this I can take you to new heights and new challenges in your relationship with Me." That alone is worthy of your reflection. The process I'm describing requires a great deal of genuine honesty, humility, and brokenness before God.

Ultimately, the path to healing is to follow Christ's example. "When they hurled their insults at him, he did not retaliate; when he suffered, he made no threats. Instead, he entrusted himself to him who judges justly" (1 Peter 2:23). This may be a worn-out cliché but it's true: You have to give it to God.

A young boy brought up in the public housing projects of Chicago received Christ as his Savior through the effective witness of some of our people at Moody Church. Later, when he was explaining what happened to him, he said to a friend, "Jesus pulled all the sins out of my heart!" What a descriptive way to put it! So I must ask: Are you willing today to let Jesus pull that offense out of your heart?

Resist moving on to the next chapter until you've truly wrestled with the answer to that question. God will be faithful. He will meet you in your pain.

A PRAYER FOR THE WOUNDED

Father, I must ask, who is able to go into the deepest places of my heart? Who is able to probe my conscience, to reveal my sin? Who is able, Father, to pull the offenses out of my heart? Who is able to give me the strength to go to those whom I have wronged, or those who have injured me? Who, O Father, who is able to do that? I cannot do this alone. Come to me at this moment. Set me free. I need Your help. I need to be broken and yielded. Grant to me all of these things, I ask. And don't stop working. Only by Your grace can I move beyond where I am at. In Jesus' name I pray. Amen.

MEET CAIN THE

THE FIRST OFFSPRING in this world was Cain: "Adam lay with his wife Eve, and she became pregnant and gave birth to Cain" (Genesis 4:1). Adam and Eve were the first parents to raise a Cain, but they were not the last. Cain represents those individuals I call *destroyers*; the kind of people who can leave you bleeding along the road and walk away feeling sorry for themselves.

Perhaps the most compelling modern-day Cain was Timothy James McVeigh—the young man who killed 168 innocent people when he blew up the Alfred P. Murrah Federal Building in Oklahoma City on April 19, 1995. His motive? To defend the Constitution, he said, and to inflict destructive injury on the American government. He walked away feeling no remorse. None whatsoever. He went to his execution firmly convinced he had done nothing that warranted regret. He died as defiantly as he had lived. Timothy McVeigh was a modern-day Cain—a destroyer.

But don't be fooled. It's easy to see that a man who wantonly kills innocent civilians is a destroyer, but so is the abuser who teaches Sunday school and the man who seeks to create dissension in a church because his wife has been removed from the church staff. And so is the woman who uses her sexuality to lure men to bed only to expose them later as another trophy of her sexual prowess.

Destroyers are found everywhere: They are found in Christian homes, in churches, and at the office. Most surprising, some are charming, helpful, and delightfully pleasant. But when they have an opportunity—particularly if they feel that their image or authority is attacked—they will destroy anyone who stands in their path. They are obsessed with self-protection and will manipulate, threaten, and distort, yet they feel no guilt. They believe that the entire world should gladly stoop to serve them, and they let everyone know why. Just look up the word *sociopath* in the dictionary, and you will find a description of some people I have met.

A destroyer is the kind of person for whom appearances are everything. Manipulative, ruthless, insidious, and murderous, he will work against you, lie to your face, and chisel away at your emotional core until you are totally diminished spiritually, emotionally, and at times, physically. Destroying others guarantees his sense of self-worth. A destroyer can hurt you deeply yet feel no sympathy. A destroyer is actually incapable of feeling hurt for anybody else, yet is keenly aware of the emotional pain he himself carries.

Stories of these kinds of people are legion. I know of a man who abandoned his wife and two-year-old daughter. Twenty years later he waltzed back into their lives and expected to give his daughter's hand in marriage and march her down the aisle of the church. When his daughter refused him because of his abandonment, he was shocked. Deeply hurt, he couldn't understand why she would do something so insensitive. He had no empathy for the pain he had caused, only a keen sense of his own feelings of rejection.

HOW TO RECOGNIZE A DESTROYER

On the outside, a destroyer may seem charming and helpful. But when the destroyer feels under attack, the person will attack anyone in his or her way. Here are the telltale marks of a destroyer:

- He will threaten and manipulate to protect his plans and interests.
- He will feel no guilt or sense of wrong for his actions.
- He will lie to your face.
- She will wear down your emotions until you feel totally diminished spiritually, emotionally, and at times, physically.
- She expects others to serve her and resents when they do not.
- She is sensitive to her own feelings of rejection yet unaware of the pain she causes.

That's precisely how a destroyer operates. And that's the problem with Cain.

THE CAIN YOU KNOW

Though a familiar Old Testament story, the Cain and Abel episode provides remarkably compelling insights into the nature of a destroyer. Not surprisingly, the first family that lived on planet Earth was dysfunctional. Read carefully through this narrative as if you're reading it for the very first time.

Adam lay with his wife Eve, and she became pregnant and gave birth to Cain. She said, "With the help of the LORD I brought forth a man." Later she gave birth to his brother Abel.

Now Abel kept flocks, and Cain worked the soil. In the course of time Cain brought some of the fruits of the soil as an offering to the LORD. But Abel brought fat portions from some of the firstborn of his flock. The LORD looked with favor on Abel and his offering, but on Cain and his offering he did not look with favor. So Cain was very angry, and his face was downcast.

Then the LORD said to Cain, "Why are you angry? Why is your face downcast? If you do what is right, will you not be accepted? But if you do not do what is right, sin is crouching at your door; it desires to have you, but you must master it."

Now Cain said to his brother Abel, "Let's go out to the field." And while they were in the field, Cain attacked his brother Abel and killed him. (Genesis 4:1–8)

The story begins happily. A baby is born to the world's first couple, and the mother and father are overjoyed. Often the future of a child does not end in the way in which his parents would have hoped or in the way in which her parents had prayed. Eve has no idea that the child she nurses so tenderly will become the world's first murderer. She does not know that he will go down in history as a poster boy for a child gone bad; she does not know that he will be referred to centuries later as one who "was of that wicked one."

Mercifully, God hides from parents the future of the child they hold in their arms. In some instances the future will be bright and hopeful; in other instances it would be dark and foreboding. Neither the mother of Judas nor the mother of Adolph Hitler knew the fate of the child they so loved and nurtured. Many a parent has experienced the heartache and anguish of hoping for an Abel, but raising a Cain. This boy will inflict horror and pain on the family because that is what destroyers do.

ANGER THAT LEADS TO THE UNTHINKABLE

Through a series of events, Cain fell out of favor with the Lord, while his brother found favor with the Lord. And the anger that welled up in Cain's heart drove him to do the unthinkable—he killed his brother in cold blood.

Why this anger on the part of Cain? I believe it to be the result of a profound sense of rejection. Notice the similarity between these two brothers. They had the same parents, respectable occupations, both brought an offering, and both gave sacrificially of what they possessed. Yet one was accepted and the other was rejected. We only wonder at the reason.

Some people believe the reason is that Abel's offering required the shedding of blood. Cain's gift consisted of a grain offering, which did not include the death of an animal. He brought the fruit of the ground. But probably more important than what Cain brought was the *attitude* with which he brought it. "By faith Abel offered God a better sacrifice than Cain did" (Hebrews 11:4a).

He chose to not offer God the best. He came to the Lord with a disobedient heart. Like the boy made to behave, Cain was in effect saying, "Dad, I want you to know that I may be sitting down on the outside, but I'm standing up on the inside!" He complied, yes, but not with an attitude of faith but of rebellion. The Bible says in 1 Peter 5:5 that "God opposes the proud but gives grace to the humble."

Clearly, Abel went to great lengths to slaughter choice animals from his flocks and then humbly brought to the Lord the fat portions—the very best he could offer. Cain simply did his duty. God rejected his offering and it made him angry; angry enough to drive him to commit premeditated murder!

Most family feuds are fueled by anger and resentment from alienated siblings. One child is perceived as being the favorite. Perhaps Abel was the favorite son, though the Scriptures don't suggest that specifically. Yet, clearly, God favored Abel and his offering over Cain and his offering. Whatever the reason, God's favoritism for Abel was the root of jealousy, envy, and anger in Cain's heart. Cain's jealousy drove him to a murderous end. And he became the epitome of a destroyer.

CHARACTERISTICS OF A CAIN

Destroyers like Cain have some very distinct characteristics. Examining these with honesty will help you understand what you might be up against in attempting reconciliation. It might also help you to ask the question: Do I have some of the characteristics of Cain?

1. The Destroyer Refuses Counsel

As pastors we've all had the experience of someone coming to us for counseling regarding a specific problem, often a marital crisis. When my schedule has seemed too busy, I've often explained that there are other pastors on our staff who are better counselors than I am, and I've encouraged the person to see one of them. But sometimes they insist—"No, I want to see *you.*"

Now imagine for a moment that people were to sign up for a counseling session, not with a flawed pastor like myself, but actually with God! You can imagine how quickly the time slots would be taken up if God were to set up counseling at the church one afternoon a week! The Almighty Himself!

Cain had that privilege! In fact, he didn't even have to sign up; God gave him counsel whether he asked for it or not. In one of the most remarkable encounters between a man and God in all of Scripture, Cain directly dialogues with God about the business of the offering and its implications. Let's read the Scripture again:

Then the LORD said to Cain, "Why are you angry? Why is your face downcast? If you do what is right, will you not be accepted? But if you do not do what is right, sin is crouching at your door; it desires to have you, but you must master it." (verses 6–7)

Obviously, Cain had failed to hide his feelings. I knew a man who could never hide his anger. He was seldom angry, but when he was, he wore it on his face. Everyone knew that for the whole day we'd have to walk on eggshells around this guy. Cain couldn't hide his anger either, and God knew that Cain's anger made him vulnerable to the Enemy's attack. God said, in effect, "Your anger is caused by sin which is crouching at your door ready to pounce on you and cause harm to you and to everyone around you."

That expression, "crouching at the door" is related to an Acadian word which means *demon*. That's why some Jewish versions of the Old Testament translate that phrase: "Sin is the demon at the door." God offered Cain some free and pretty reliable advice. He'd better master that raging emotion or it would be his undoing. Cain did not want mastery over his sin. "Whereas Eve had to be talked into her sin by the serpent, it appears that Cain would not be talked out of his intended sin, even by the Lord himself."[1]

Cain flatly rejected God's counsel, disregarded the warning, and went out and murdered his brother. So much for counseling! A destroyer always disregards wise counsel. He sings the sentiments of Frank Sinatra: "I'll do it my way!"

Have you ever tried to reason with a person who is at root

a destroyer? A married woman trusted her mother-in-law with some personal information in a candid discussion they had about their past, etc. Sometime later this mother-in-law left her married son a shocking voice mail suggesting that he divorce his wife (the daughter-in-law). The angry voice mail explained that the son should divorce his wife considering her past and that she was "unworthy" of her son.

As things ensued, matters discussed in confidence were not only made public but also exaggerated, twisted, and taken out of context. Turns out that the son—thankfully—was not surprised by all of this. He knew his mother as angry, manipulative, and obsessively controlling. She was opposed to him marrying because she would lose control of him and he would not be around to run her errands and fix the house when it needed it. In short, she wanted to destroy their marriage in order to "get her son back" under her thumb. She was willing to destroy a happy marriage if only it gave her a measure of regained control.

She had few friends because she treated all of them the same way: They existed only to affirm her view of other people and the world in general. Everyone she met was either all right or all wrong, and she was the sole judge. There could be no compromise; you either saw reality as she did or you were *persona non grata*. No wonder her husband had long since retreated into his shell and passively refused to offer opinions about anything that mattered. The price for peace was a silent, if bitter, yielding to whatever came out of this woman's mouth.

How would you like to counsel a woman like this? Let out a sigh of relief because you won't have that opportunity, since people like this never seek counseling, though they recommend it for others. Why should those whose attitudes and views are so right—in their minds, at least—go for help? Perhaps the son and daughter-in-law need counseling, but not her. Nevertheless, we must treat people like this with tenderness, knowing that there are reasons for their pain. Yet, sadly, even if God spoke to her as definitely as He did to Cain, it is unlikely that she would heed His warning.

Destroyers are not interested in truth; they are only interested in proclaiming their own version of it. Some destroyers believe that the world should stoop to gladly serve them and their most cherished dreams; others believe that they are God's gift of justice to set things right in this crooked world. So they gladly volunteer their services for the task.

They are not prone to take advice, for no one is wiser than they.

2. The Destroyer Avoids Responsibility

Cain patently avoids taking responsibility for his actions. When God asks him where his brother is, the Almighty is trying to elicit some confession, some acknowledgment of wrongdoing.

"I don't know," Cain answers. The young man lied. He played ignorant and then sneered, asking, "Am I my brother's keeper?" The right answer to that question is, "Yes." You do have responsibility for your brother. But Cain, of course, doesn't see life that way.

A destroyer routinely lashes out at others, while he refuses to own his part in the matter. A destroyer will lie, twist, and distort the truth. At every turn he avoids taking responsibility for his actions and denies the need for mutual accountability. So for Cain to give such an incredulous response betrays the true condition of his heart. He was in rebellion against God.

Cain couldn't hide. God said to him, "Your brother's blood cries out to me from the ground." One commentator has said that this is one of the most monumental statements in Scripture. "It needs no explanation but retains validity throughout all the centuries . . . the most important phrase is 'to me.' The blood of the victim cries out and there is someone to whom it cries out. Cain cannot hide his deed."[2]

No matter how hard Cain attempts to avoid responsibility, he cannot hide his sin from God. His brother's blood cried out in judgment against him.

A church member who posed as an investment broker was able to attract a great deal of business from Christians who trusted him. Some transferred their annuities and bank accounts to this man's firm, and he produced reports that showed a growing profit.

Within time, the people learned that they'd been swindled; the reports were bogus and their money was gone. The man had squandered the money on his own private projects and had nothing to show for the hundreds of thousands of dollars he'd been entrusted with.

Yes, he was tried for fraud and served a brief time in jail, but he is now free, and the people who invested with him are minus their retirement funds and savings. Some have had to declare bankruptcy.

Most remarkably—though not surprisingly—the man

offered no apology to those he had so cruelly and deliberately wronged. Even the plight of widows who were now bereft of savings did not elicit a word of sympathy. He was, however, known to be quite upset with his lot in life, protesting that he had intended to invest the money, that it was other people's fault that he'd not done so, etc.

Destroyers shift blame; they do not take personal responsibility for the evil they perpetuate. Reconciliation with them is, of course, seldom possible.

3. The Destroyer Has a Self-Absorbed Life

The third characteristic of a destroyer is complete self-absorption. Once God delivered judgment, Cain began to whine. Here's how Eugene Peterson paraphrases Cain's self-absorbed response: "Cain said to God, 'My punishment is too much. I can't take it! You've thrown me off the land and I can never again face you. I'm a homeless wanderer on Earth and whoever finds me will kill me.'" (THE MESSAGE)

Makes you want to cry for him!

There is no thought given to the pain inflicted on his brother when he was killed and no apology to his parents who sorrowed because of their oldest son's crime. Cain's entire focus is on his own plight as a wanderer and a fugitive. He bemoans the possibility that someone will do to him what he did to his brother.

Paranoia also sets in as Cain becomes convinced everyone is out to get him. "Whoever finds me will kill me." The self-absorbed person, even when found guilty, feels sorry for only himself because he alone is standing against an unjust world.

Destroyers play by a different set of rules. There is plenty of sorrow for themselves but none for those they've injured.

A Chicago police officer told me that among all the horrible things he's witnessed over the years, the most difficult to understand is when a teenager kills another teenager and then goes out to dinner with his family, as if absolutely nothing happened. Destroyers are so self-absorbed in their own pain they've grown numb to the pain of others. Though keenly aware of their own hurt, they are incapable of feeling sympathy for their victims.

CLOSER TO HOME

Now you may have never killed anyone or, for that matter, even been tempted to. And it's likely you're not guilty of anything like I've described here in order to illustrate my point. But you may be wondering if you could possibly be a destroyer-type person. It doesn't take much bitterness or pent-up anger to lash out at someone you love and cause lifelong injury. Perhaps you have had a difficult time accepting the hard truth about yourself, or receiving loving but honest advice about the way you are living. You may also be realizing your tendency to shift the blame for your actions to others, choosing to maintain a victim mentality.

To bring this down to where we live: We can destroy people in smaller ways, but ways that are just as sure. We can be destroyers with our words, with our attitudes, and with our critical spirit. You need to be honest enough to face just how difficult you are to live with. Don't be too quick to hang the observations of this chapter on everyone but yourself. You may be a prime candidate for that one-on-one counseling with God that Cain so recklessly spurned. Don't make his mistake.

LIFE-CHANGING LESSONS

A pastor had a clock in his office that was well-known for its inability to keep time; sometimes it was too fast, sometimes too slow. He put a sign under it: "This clock is not dependable; don't blame the hands, the trouble is deeper." Our trouble is deeper than we imagine it to be, but God can change us from the inside out.

Regardless of whether you are the victim or the perpetrator, I want to offer you some practical lessons from the tragedy of Cain.

First, *either we will master sin or sin will master us.*

Just like with Cain, sin is crouching at the door of your heart too. If you disregard God's counsel, you may become an easy target for a demon at the door. The apostle John warned believers, "Do not be like Cain, who belonged to the evil one and murdered his brother. And why did he murder him? Because his own actions were evil and his brother's were righteous" (1 John 3:12). God held Cain responsible for his own action, even though he had made himself vulnerable to the Devil.

All Cain needed was a fit of jealousy to destroy his brother. To put it plainly, "the Devil got him!" Sin was crouching at the door and pounced! Unless you open yourself continually to the work of the Holy Spirit and allow Him to control your thoughts and motives, you too can play into the Devil's hands. Sin will master you and eventually destroy you.

Remember, the purpose of the cross was to destroy the works of the Devil (1 John 3:8). Those sins that want to destroy you must be humbly brought into the presence of Christ who can set us free from the anger that leads to vengeance and "getting even." Satan is ready to pounce, but we can participate in the victory of Jesus over him and his lies.

If you do not master your bitterness and anger, it will master you!

Second, *we can be healed by the blood that forgives.*

Jesus offers to us "the sprinkled blood that speaks a better word than the blood of Abel" (Hebrews 12:24). Abel's blood cried out words of judgment against Cain and all who would choose his sinful ways. The blood of Jesus offers words of forgiveness and reconciliation to all who embrace the cross. At the foot of the cross both destroyer and victim can come together and find healing.

Families can be reconciled as each confesses his or her sin —as each one owns their part in the breakdown. And I'm not just writing to the Cains who are reading this chapter, but also to the Abels, the man who was a victim of his brother's anger. Abel, of course, died, but you are alive and perhaps living with the pain of someone else's wrong.

Healing is found in the One whose blood offers forgiveness, not judgment. And total forgiveness can be yours in Christ. And if someone approaches you and says, "You know you really hurt me," let them own their feelings. That's where true reconciliation begins.

A PRAYER FOR FORGIVENESS AND GRACE

Father, bring to mind the people whom we have hurt—either intentionally or unintentionally. Help us to be honest and open to Your Holy Spirit to show us the full impact of our words and actions. Forgive us for our own callousness and grant us the grace to make things right with those whose hearts we have wounded. Make us sensitive and thoughtful, esteeming others better than ourselves. Let us respond to our hurt in such a way that You receive glory. We pray in Jesus' name. Amen.

FAMILIES AT

WHEN TRUST
FAILS

JIM, IN ANGER, REBUKED his daughter Janet for her part in a family feud. She felt unfairly attacked and believed that the blame lay elsewhere, namely with her father's wife (that is, her mother). Soon the feud spread to all the children and grandchildren, and, yes, even Jim's parents took sides. There seemed to be no way to resolve the matter for the simple reason that each kept insisting that someone else was at fault.

No one, to my mind, was trying to be deceitful, but each was convinced about the rightness of his or her position. The standoff continued for months, until someone stepped back and reconsidered the situation and made a very difficult decision: to admit guilt even when he was convinced that the major fault really lay with another member of the family.

That family member was wise. There are times when we have to humble ourselves to go beyond self-justification. I'm not suggesting that we should ever be dishonest and admit to things we have not done. I am suggesting that when we are willing to deal with our part in the feud, no matter how minor (in our eyes), it often breaks the logjam and begins the process of reconciliation. Our humility is often the bridge over which others will pass to extend reconciliation to others.

Of course, how we admit to our part in the breach of fellowship has to be carefully considered. If a wife is trying to reconcile with an abusive husband, he may take the confession, twist it, blame her for everything, and say, "See, I told you it was all your fault."

There are those who want us to admit our guilt so that we again come under their control. Or they have demands and expectations that far exceed what we can honestly give them. Reconciliation can only take place on their unreasonable terms.

The family, I think, is the crucible in which the most intimate and potentially devastating relationships occur. It is the environment in which we learn our identity and our self-worth—it is there we find ultimate acceptance, emotional care, and nurturing. But because so much is riding on the family, it has also become the place of enormous conflict. Nowhere is reconciliation more needed and nowhere is it more difficult to attain.

Jealousy, I suspect, has torn apart more family relationships than any other single factor. As a pastor, I've witnessed it more times than I can count. And by the time the fractured families come to me, the damage often is deep, and the prognosis for recovery bleak.

Inheritance and money can cause deep rifts in families too. Recently, I was talking to a young couple in financial need, and they had been invited to live in the home of his parents. What they discovered, though, was that his parents harbored serious hidden agendas. Intense conflicts arose quickly. Unfortunately, as the strife intensified, the son took sides with his parents and alienated his wife. Can a wife ever recover from the pain suffered when her own husband refuses to defend her?

Thankfully, God desires to bring healing. The Bible helps us with real-life examples of His provision during times of family pain. Perhaps the most compelling story about family strife is the story of Jacob and Esau. What sparks flew in that home! Still, God in His goodness came through with unexpected peace and healing. In the process of taking a look at this family feud we shall learn some lessons about how to initiate forgiveness and reconciliation. We shall also discover that God is often gracious even to a dysfunctional family.

Your reconciliation to your brother is important to God. In fact, He says it is a matter of urgency. Jesus said, "Therefore, if you are offering your gift at the altar and there remember that your brother has something against you, leave your gift there in front of the altar. First go and be reconciled to your brother; then come and offer your gift" (Matthew 5:23–24). Jesus is saying whether you are the offender or the offended, your gift means nothing if you have not attempted reconciliation. Whether it is a member of your biological family or the family of God, Christ wants us to restore our relationships.

So let's turn to the Scriptures to see how two estranged brothers were eventually brought together. There are times when even frayed family relationships become opportunities for God to demonstrate His power and grace. Though all conflict is rooted in the self-serving nature of sin, God can use such circumstances to glorify Himself.

DOUBLE TROUBLE

The story, found in Genesis 25, begins in the heart of a beautiful, godly woman named Rebekah. She was barren and desperately desired a child. Her husband asked God to bless them with a child, and God gave him more than he asked for. She conceived twins. But even in the womb there was a hint of the family's stormy future. The Scriptures explain that "the babies jostled each other within her" (Genesis 25:22). Rebekah prayed and asked the Lord the meaning of her jostling twins, to which the Lord replied with a remarkable explanation. "Two nations are in your womb, and two peoples from within you will be separated; one people will be stronger than the other, and the older will serve the younger" (verse 23).

In other words, the two boys represent a world of conflict and a lifetime of struggle! Not the best news for a young mother to receive. But that's the backdrop for this amazing story. It is a classic story of conflict, deception, and reconciliation.

The fact that God said the older son would serve the younger represented a turn of the tables from how things normally operated. Firstborns always anticipated the inheritance and the blessing associated with it; older sons, not the younger ones, were obliged to pass on the family line. Yet here the older would serve the younger.

Even in their physical characteristics we see the potential for conflict. When Esau was born, he came out "red, and his whole body was like a hairy garment," hence his name (verse 25; "hairy" was a Hebrew pun on the name "Esau"). The second-born was Jacob, who came forth with "his hand grasping Esau's heel." Jacob literally means "the supplanter" or "wrestler." You get the picture! The younger son from his first actions showed his true colors. He was a "heel grabber," taking hold of his older brother. From the outset it would be a wrestling match!

BOYS WILL BE BOYS

These two brothers grew and developed in accordance with their gifting and their abilities, along with all their natural—albeit rowdy—traits! Esau became a hunter, a lover of the outdoors, and the favorite son of Isaac. Jacob preferred being at home, apparently exploring his culinary interests, and, not surprisingly, enjoying the adoration of his mother, Rebekah. The stage was set for conflict.

Two things happened that caused a division that would last for twenty years or more. The first is described in Genesis 25:

> Once when Jacob was cooking some stew, Esau came in from the open country, famished. He said to Jacob, "Quick, let me have some of that red stew! I'm famished!" (That is why he was also called Edom.)

Jacob replied, "First sell me your birthright."

"Look, I am about to die," Esau said. "What good is the birthright to me?"

But Jacob said, "Swear to me first." So he swore an oath to him, selling his birthright to Jacob.

Then Jacob gave Esau some bread and some lentil stew. He ate and drank, and then got up and left.

So Esau despised his birthright. (verses 29–34)

Esau was hungry and wanted to eat, no matter what. He who had no interests beyond his immediate needs, sold his birthright to his younger brother. Sadly, he sacrificed the permanent on the altar of the immediate. The owner of the birthright would receive a double portion of the estate and have the legal continuation of the family line. He fell into Jacob's trap. That's incident number one.

Incident number two has to do with the father, Isaac. He thought he was going to die, though he actually lived many more years. Yet, his obsession with his own death set the next crippling episode in motion. In Genesis 27, we're told Isaac believed his days on earth were short and called his son Esau to his side to request a specially prepared meal of fresh game. Then he promised that he would give his blessing to Esau. Rebekah overheard the conversation, and after Esau had left on his hunting expedition, she conspired with her beloved son, Jacob, to trick Isaac into offering the blessing to him, instead. Her plan was to disguise Jacob as Esau, prepare a scrumptious meal, and trick the old man into pronouncing the blessing upon Jacob. The plan worked almost flawlessly, but not without Jacob lying outright to his old father's face!

Jacob said to his father, "I am Esau, your firstborn." The old man asked, "Who are you?" And he said, "I am Esau." Lie number *one*.

Then Isaac said, "How did you get the game so quickly?" He answered, "Well, the Lord has blessed me." Lie number *two*.

And then he said, "Well, you know you have the voice of Jacob. Come near me." After feeling the fake fur on Jacob's arm, Isaac asked again, "Are you really my son Esau?" Jacob answered, "Yes, I am." Lie number *three*. (See verses 18–24.)

The blessing went to Jacob—just as the Lord had predicted, "The older will serve the younger." But Esau was enraged when he discovered how he had been defrauded. When the old man, Isaac, found out what happened, he nearly lost his mind. He does give a blessing of sorts to Esau but it was too little, too late. Now you have a whole lot of trouble under one roof because of a deceptive plan to steal God's blessing. The result was a fractured family with multiple wrongs suffered.

We read ominously, "So Esau hated Jacob . . ." (verse 41 NKJV).

Need more be said?

WHAT GOES AROUND, COMES AROUND

So Jacob received through manipulation and deceit what God intended to give him anyway! After all, the blessing was promised to be his. If he had waited, God would have worked it out some other way, without Jacob's deceit. But he wanted to do things his way.

So when Jacob and Rebekah took matters into their own

hands, the family was left in ruins. As a result, Esau hated Jacob and planned to murder him. This might have been the Cain/Abel scenario all over again. Except this time, Jacob would have been partly to blame because he and their mother fomented Esau's hostility through their manipulation and deceit.

Once again, Rebekah intervened. She persuaded Jacob to leave home and live with his uncle, Laban, Rebekah's brother. There the pattern of deception and manipulation continued, until Jacob met his match in Laban, an experienced cheater and master deceiver! You might say they engaged in "mutually agreed deception."

Jacob fell immediately in love with Laban's daughter Rachel and agreed to work seven years for Laban in exchange for her hand in marriage. After the seven years had passed, however, Laban tricked Jacob, and gave Jacob his daughter Leah instead. (Clearly Laban heeded the custom of having the bride completely veiled during the ceremony!) Eventually, Jacob did marry Rachel also, but she came with a heavy price: seven more years of working for his father-in-law! Apparently, though, all that sufficed to teach Jacob a valuable lesson: God gives the blessing; you cannot bless yourself.

THE LONG ROAD BACK HOME— STEPS TOWARD RECONCILIATION

Finally, the Lord convinced Jacob of his need to return to his homeland and face his past. As always, God initiated the reconciliation. That's a good principle to remember when you're facing a conflict of your own. Even when a relationship seems broken beyond repair, God may lead you in taking steps toward reconciliation. I believe that's precisely what He did in Jacob's life. He told him to return home and promised, "I will be with you."

On his journey home, Jacob realized he would soon come face-to-face with his estranged brother. And since he was clearly the guilty party, he assumed Esau would retaliate for Jacob's deeds. Full of fear, Jacob prepared a reconciliation plan. Yet God intervened with a plan of His own. Remarkably, Genesis 32:1 explains that "Jacob also went on his way, and the angels of God met him." What an unexpected surprise! God always stands on the side of anyone who rightfully pursues reconciliation. And because God was in it, Jacob's path toward reconciliation provides some critical steps for anyone to follow who wants to reconcile with a loved one or friend.

1. Offer a Gesture of Genuine Goodwill

To his everlasting credit, Jacob offered his brother a gesture of goodwill. He sent messengers ahead to tell Esau that he was prepared to greet him and give to him a generous gift.

> Jacob sent messengers ahead of him to his brother Esau in the land of Seir, the country of Edom. He instructed them: "This is what you are to say to my master Esau: 'Your servant Jacob says, I have been staying with Laban and have remained there till now. I have cattle and donkeys, sheep and goats, menservants and maidservants. Now I am sending this message to my lord, that I may find favor in your eyes.'" (Genesis 32:3–5)

Sometimes making a personal sacrifice for the sake of the broken relationship can begin the healing process. Here was a step in practical humility that would disarm Esau and prepare both of their hearts for reconciliation.

I know a family that for years was broken apart over business disagreements. Three brothers and their respective families were torn to pieces over misunderstandings and deception. The two younger brothers opposed the oldest who they believed had conned them out of tens of thousands of dollars. Even though the accusations were false, the older brother, desperate to be reconciled to his family, willingly paid to his younger siblings an astounding amount of money—money he knew rightfully belonged to him. The sacrifice was worth the opportunity to be restored to his family. That genuine gesture of goodwill—painful as it was—acted like a splint to allow the healing process to begin. In a family standoff, someone has to break the impasse.

When Jacob's servants returned, they told him Esau was coming with four hundred men. Jacob's fear intensified. Which led him to his second step—prayer.

2. Humble Yourself before God

Jacob had chosen to humble himself in anticipation of meeting his brother, but now he humbled himself in the presence of God. He prayed with intensity:

> O God of my father Abraham, God of my father Isaac, O LORD, who said to me, "Go back to your country and your relatives, and I will make you prosper," I am

unworthy of all the kindness and faithfulness you have
shown your servant. . . . Save me, I pray, from the hand
of my brother Esau. (Genesis 32:9–11)

Prayer, desperate prayer, seems so simple, but it's a step rarely
taken by those in family conflict. In my many years of pastoral
ministry, I've personally witnessed the power of prayer in bringing otherwise irreconcilable parties together. Jacob called on the
Lord for help and asked that he would find favor with Esau.
What a tremendous prayer! He pleaded with God as he had
never prayed before that his brother's heart would be softened.

God now initiated an event that would place Jacob in a
wrestling match—a wrestling match with none other than
God Himself! Jacob would now experience God in a way far
beyond his previous encounters. After hearing that Esau and
his forces were drawing near, he sent his family and servants
on to a place of safety while he remained at the brook of
Jabbok. There, the Bible says, Jacob wrestled with an angel
until daybreak. (See Genesis 32:24 ff.)

Finally, the angel touched Jacob's hip socket and crippled
him. That touch was so powerful, so debilitating that Jacob
realized he was in the presence of God. And with that, the
heavenly visitor appeared to want to leave and said, "Let me
go, for it is daybreak." But that's what prompted Jacob to say,
"I will not let you go unless you bless me." That was Jacob's
way—trying to secure a blessing for himself, but this time he
was rightly trying to secure it from God Himself. Yes, the angel
was the Lord, most probably the second member of the Trinity,
the Lord Jesus.

And then the angel asked Jacob, "What is your name?" He answered, "Jacob." If we remember that Jacob's name means "cheater," in saying his own name, Jacob in effect admitted to the Lord all his years of trying to lie and cheat and sucker his way into securing the blessing that was already his. In response to admitting he was *Jacob*, God changed his name to *Israel* because he had "struggled with God and with men and have overcome."

He then left to meet his brother, physically weak but spiritually strong. "His carnal weapons were lame and useless; they failed him in his contest with God. What he had surmised for the past twenty years now dawned on him: he was in the hands of the One against whom it is useless to struggle."[1]

Self-sufficiency is incompatible with the work of God in any age. Crippled in weakness, he now has to become bold in faith.

God allowed Jacob's circumstances to spiral so out of control that he was in effect forced to humiliation and great need. Jacob would not be able now to depend on any human strength as he left to meet Esau. He went limping, clearly unable to wrestle with his brother if it should come to that. He left with his blessing which was a new sense of total dependence upon God. And that's the way of genuine biblical reconciliation. Whether it's Paul's thorn in the flesh, or an illness, or a financial dilemma impossible to overcome, God always uses those situations to humble and weaken those whom He intends to bless.

WHAT THE BIBLE SAYS ABOUT RECONCILIATION

The Scriptures are very clear about our need to reconcile with those we have offended. Here are some key injunctions for restoring relationships after an offense exists:

- *"If you are offering your gift at the altar and there remember that your brother has something against you, leave your gift . . . go and be reconciled to your brother; then come and offer your gift"* (Matthew 5:23–24). We can worship God effectively only after we have mended any tear between ourselves and someone else.
- *"Humble yourselves before the Lord, and he will lift you up"* (James 4:10). When we ask forgiveness, we are humbling ourselves, knowing not only are we admitting our responsibility but that our request for forgiveness may be rejected. Yet God promises He will exalt us for our effort. (See also 1 Peter 5:6.)
- *"God, who reconciled us to himself through Christ[,] gave us the ministry of reconciliation. . . . And he has committed to us the message of reconciliation. We are therefore Christ's ambassadors, as though God were making his appeal through us"* (2 Corinthians 5:18–20). Followers of Christ are to have ministries of reconciliation, bringing people back to God and showing reconciliation through us.
- *"For if you forgive men when they sin against you, your heavenly Father will also forgive you. But if you do not forgive men their sins, your Father will not forgive your sins"* (Matthew 6:14–15). We are to forgive in order to maintain fellowship with our Father. Our unwillingness to restore broken relationships can damage our relationship with God.

3. *Humbling Yourself before Your Adversary*

The third and final step in the process of reconciliation is humbling yourself before the one to whom you seek restoration. That's what Jacob did before Esau.

Jacob had learned the blessing of humbling himself before the Lord. Proverbs 15:33 says, "The fear of the LORD teaches a man wisdom, and humility comes before honor." Throughout most of his life, Jacob had it backwards. In his whole life he wanted honor before humility and that brought him nothing but heartache. Humility is one of the essential ingredients of genuine biblical reconciliation. It is the stuff of healed relationships.

And so Jacob, wounded by his wrestling match, limped to meet Esau and knelt before him seven times (Genesis 33:3). We can only imagine the scene—as this once conniving brother humbled himself before the brother from whom he stole his father's blessing. Instead of retaliating, Esau, the offended brother, runs and embraces his younger brother. And so Jacob and Esau were reconciled. A magnificent portrait of God's grace and power!

After Jacob's family is appropriately introduced to Esau, Jacob insists that Esau keep the gifts intended for him. Jacob says, "For to see your face is like seeing the face of God, now that you have received me favorably" (verse 10). Note well that the forgiving person reflects the nature of God.

I wish we could say that the brothers were fully reconciled to one another. At first it appears as if they were, for Esau says to Jacob, "Let us be on our way; I'll accompany you" (verse 12). But Jacob does not accept his brother's suggestion, but encourages

Esau to go on ahead of him because the small children and the nursing cattle would not be able to keep up. Jacob does promise, however, that they will eventually meet back in Mount Seir where Esau lives.

But although Esau went back to Mount Seir, Jacob did not. "So that day Esau started on his way back to Seir. Jacob, however, went to Succoth, where he built a place for himself and made shelters for his livestock" (verses 16–17). The brothers, so far as we know, never met again, except for their father Isaac's funeral (Genesis 35:29), which is the only place where many estranged relatives meet.

Mistrust sometimes results in partial reconciliation, which may be defined as an understood agreement to keep a cordial distance between one another; it is an attempt to ask and receive formal forgiveness, without enjoying fellowship with one another. Sometimes it is the kind of relationship enjoyed by brothers, one of whom is a Christian and the other is not.

There are many families who never experience even a basic level of God's reconciliation. Many broken, bitter, angry people go to their graves with a wrong never made right, or an injustice never answered. We must trust God even with those sadder endings, but the story of Jacob and Esau does offer hope to anyone struggling through a family conflict. And it provides a couple of extremely valuable lessons, as well.

TRANSFORMING LESSONS

Here are some practical lessons from the war and uneasy peace between Jacob and Esau. These are lessons in trust and reconciliation we can all apply.

First, *mistrust sometimes necessitates that we set boundaries to keep some people from constantly sowing discord in our lives.*

When Jacob and Laban separated, they agreed to draw a line in the dirt and promised that neither would cross the agreed boundary (Genesis 31:45–50). One woman, whose mother constantly was disrupting her husband and family, had to insist that Grandma not see her own grandchildren. The daughter and her husband became weary of the manipulation, the angry voice mails, and the continual expectations of an obsessive/compulsive mother who for years had effectively used guilt to get her own way. When possible, put barriers around yourself and the toxic people who subtly inflict their harmful influence on you or members of your family.

There are some people whom you will never fully trust. Why? Because they will only reconcile on their terms; you have to admit your offenses but they will never admit to theirs, and if they do it is to something very minor. They might profess to want reconciliation, but only if their antagonist comes under their authority. Like a daughter said of her overbearing, controlling mother, "She owns the Midwest distributorship for guilt and manipulation." To try to develop the relationship is like pouring water on silk flowers.

Second, *God sometimes uses a crooked stick to make a straight line.*

Think about this: Who would you prefer as a neighbor, Jacob or Esau? Perhaps Esau would be the better neighbor, because he might not have been as deceiving as Jacob. Yet, incredibly we read, "Esau I have hated, and I have turned his mountains into a wasteland and left his inheritance to the desert jackals" (Malachi 1:3). Ultimately, God pronounced judgment on Esau and his lineage, and blessed Jacob instead.

Jacob the deceiver is the one who receives the blessing and through him the line of the Messiah is preserved; he was a crooked stick but with him God drew the next link in salvation history. At times God uses a crooked stick to make a straight line. He used Esau to teach Jacob some lessons, but Jacob would be the one through whom the blessing comes. After all, "the older will serve the younger."

You say, "You don't know my brother. He's a rascal and he's immature and he doesn't fear the Lord. There's no way we could ever be reconciled." The story of Jacob and Esau—and the way God not only worked in Jacob's heart but also Esau's —offers another hope for a meaningful meeting of the minds, if not full reconciliation. No one is beyond God's gracious reach. There's no heart too stubborn, too rebellious, or too angry to heal. And that leads me to the third important lesson.

Third, *true reconciliation is God's work.*

God first reconciles us to Himself, as He did Jacob. The apostle Paul wrote that "all this is from God, who reconciled us to himself through Christ and gave us the ministry of reconciliation: that God was reconciling the world to himself in Christ, not counting men's sins against them" (2 Corinthians 5:18-19).

It is impossible to be reconciled fully to God without wanting to be reconciled fully to those from whom you are estranged. A Christian contractor promised his clients one kind of building material but then built their homes with inferior products. He "managed his sin" quite well until the Holy Spirit brought great conviction to his conscience. Finally, he mortgaged his house and borrowed money to pay back the profit he made with the cheaper materials. The lesson to be learned is that *the more fully we are reconciled to God, the more fully we want to be reconciled to others, regardless of the cost.*

You may be reading this book because you're desperate to be reconciled to a family member or friend. Now you're realizing you've never been reconciled to God—you are not in a right relationship with God. You can know God by trusting in Jesus, His Son, as your Savior. You can ask Him to forgive your sins and to reconcile you to God, your Creator. But that's only the beginning. Once you have restored your relationship with God, it is His will that you restore your relationship with others. That includes those you've wronged or those who have hurt or wronged you.

Are you willing to do whatever God expects you to do to restore fellowship with someone you've wronged or who has wronged you? Jesus said, "If you cannot forgive those who have wronged you, your Father can't forgive you." (See Matthew 6:14–15.) That's a sobering reality!

The Jacob and Esau story demonstrates that God is on your side when you seek reconciliation. His promise to Jacob is one for all of us: "I will be with you."

A PRAYER FOR ALL OF US

Father, we pray for those with whom we are not reconciled. In some instances we don't know even where to begin the process, but we seek Your face, asking that You might lead us as we obey You. Soften our hearts and those from whom we are estranged. May we be "quick to listen, slow to speak, and slow to wrath," we pray in Jesus' name. Amen.

DODGING SPEARS

BULLYING HAS BECOME A MAJOR PROBLEM in America's public schools. Once a basic nuisance and an expected part of everyday school life, bullying is now epidemic. School districts are developing entire programs to educate teachers and children on how to handle and deal with bullies in schools.

This is not the first time bullies have been roaming the hallways and playgrounds—many young adults today live scarred lives, carrying with them secret emotional pain from the relentless assaults and abuse they endured as schoolchildren. Maybe they suffered at the hand of some cocky, insecure kid, or perhaps it was a patrolling pack of playground bullies.

Bullies hurt—and their words and attacks can stay with you for a lifetime. The old saw about bullies can be revised:

"Sticks and stones will break my bones . . . and names will always harm me."

But there are adult bullies too. These are not physically intimidating people, sporting strange horns or wearing angry scowls on their faces. Yet they operate in offices and churches, and you might find some among your relatives. Some of you who are reading these words are married to one.

These adult bullies might more accurately be labeled *spear throwers*. They are those individuals hell-bent on damaging and threatening you—even destroying you or your reputation. Motivated by jealousy, they stop at nothing to make certain you melt into a pool of fear and shame at their words or actions. A book on the subject of overcoming wrongs would be incomplete without a discussion on the topic of spear throwers and how to deal with them from God's perspective.

Spear throwers like to see people squirm. They are self-absorbed, self-motivated, and self-deceived. And they do it all cloaked with verses of Scripture and hidden behind the loftiest motives. These people exist in offices, in neighborhoods, and sometimes within our own homes. Many of them claim deep relationship with God. They may be Sunday school teachers, social workers, and devoted parents. Amazingly, they can be caring and thoughtful—and mean and evil—all at once.

Perhaps you were surprised to learn that the family into which you married can be caring and outwardly peaceful, but also uncaring and mean. You did not know that so much evil could hide behind their closed doors. Perhaps the spear thrower is your spouse! You ask yourself, *Why does the man who threw me bouquets before we were married now throw spears my way?*

USING KINDNESS TO KILL

Spear throwers can be the most dangerous because they can use kindness to kill.

I heard a sad story about a young Bible college graduate trained as a church musician. Invited to serve in a well-known church, the young man signed on to what he believed would be his dream position—serving the Lord in music near the place where he had been raised. Not even a few days went by before he discovered the man who had recruited him and treated him with such grace and kindness was really a wolf in sheep's clothing. A spear thrower—and a remarkably skillful and subtle one at that.

The next eleven months of the young man's life and ministry were torturous as he endured the shocking disillusion of his first local church ministry gone bad, and the unspeakable pain of public criticism and ridicule at the hand of this respected pastor. Finally, literally under the cover of darkness, after only eleven months, the young man left, broken, ashamed, physically ill, and completely destroyed, never to return again. It took seven years of healing and counseling before that young man could begin to entertain the prospect of reentering the ministry. Sadly, such tragic tales abound in the church today.

Yet, in a mysterious way, God in His sovereign goodness often uses the painful and at times debilitating injury of a spear thrower to make us readier for His service. That's what I'd like to consider with you in this chapter—the lessons God would have us learn when we're pinned to the wall by a spear thrower.

APPEARANCES ARE EVERYTHING

The classic biblical illustration of a spear thrower is King Saul from the Old Testament. One thing you discover about spear throwers is that though it's not necessary for them to be good, it's essential for them to *appear* good. For Saul it was all about appearances. Yet one day Saul would literally pick up a spear and hurl it at the man who was trying to help the king.

This spear thrower had every reason in the world to enjoy his life under the full blessing and favor of the Lord, without the need for manipulation and envy. Let's consider King Saul's extraordinary positive characteristics.

First, *he was anointed by God.* Read carefully how Saul's kingly ministry began. "Then Samuel took a flask of oil and poured it on Saul's head and kissed him, saying, 'Has not the LORD anointed you leader over his inheritance?'" (1 Samuel 10:1).

God Himself, through the famed prophet Samuel, anointed Saul as leader over His chosen people. God had bestowed on him the highest honor of being anointed the very first king to lead His people. He was exalted not by men but by God.

Second, *Saul was unusually gifted.* In his case, the gift was prophecy. Samuel said to the newly appointed king, "The Spirit of the LORD will come upon you in power, and you will prophesy with them; and you will be changed into a different person. Once these signs are fulfilled, do whatever your hand finds to do, for God is with you" (1 Samuel 10:6–7). God followed through with His promise, and as Saul arrived at Gibeah, a procession of prophets met him and "the spirit of the God came upon him in power, and he joined in their prophesying" (verse 10). God gifted Saul uniquely and promised him that he would be equipped with a remarkable gift and personality.

Third, *Saul enjoyed a striking physical appearance* (note 1 Samuel 9:2). The end of chapter 10 reveals that when the people were going out to crown Saul they couldn't find him. Apparently, because of his humility he was hiding somewhere. He had that self-effacing quality that only would have made him even more attractive as a leader and king. When he finally emerged, he stood a head taller than anyone else. Tall, dark, and handsome, too!

Fourth, *Saul possessed unusual military prowess.* A close read of 1 Samuel 11 reveals Saul's military genius and courage in battle. He was God's man, for God's possession, for God's use among the people, for that moment in a nation's history.

With such a litany of accolades you'd think he'd be a model of genuine godliness and integrity. Sadly, Saul's inner character didn't match his exterior strength or giftedness. He looked great on the outside, but inside he was desperately flawed.

What pushed Saul over the edge was when someone made him look bad! First Samuel 17 records the slaying of Goliath, the defiant Philistine warrior, by a young shepherd named David. David had become a close friend with Saul's son, Jonathan. David had also become a confidant of Saul's. But David's bravery was too much for the paranoid king to bear. The multitude's exultation in David's victory over Goliath ultimately revealed Saul's flawed soul.

Whatever Saul sent him to do, David did it so success-
fully that Saul gave him a high rank in the army. This
pleased all the people, and Saul's officers as well.
When the men were returning home after David had
killed the Philistine, the women came out from all the
towns of Israel to meet King Saul with singing and
dancing, with joyful songs and with tambourines and
lutes. As the danced, they sang: "Saul has slain his
thousands, and David his tens of thousands." Saul
was very angry; this refrain galled him. "They have
credited David with tens of thousands," he thought,
"but with me only thousands. What more can he get
but the kingdom?" And from that time on Saul kept a
jealous eye on David. (1 Samuel 18:5–9)

Saul enjoyed his song, "Saul has slain his thousands," but
he hated David's song, "But David his tens of thousands."
We've all met people who are in love with their song but
despise our song. If Saul had a T-shirt it might have read,
"Worship me and we'll get along just fine!"

The next day a harmful or evil spirit from God rushed
upon Saul, and the king raved within his house while David
sat playing the lyre to calm the king's nerves. Saul had his
spear in his hand and in a jealous rage, he hurled it, hoping
to "pin David to the wall." It happened twice, though David
evaded him both times (1 Samuel 18:10–11). Saul's jealousy
had spawned a murderous pattern of spear throwing. Anointed,
called, gifted, good-looking . . . and a spear thrower. That was
Saul.

Don't be confused because this evil spirit came from the Lord. Only God could give this spirit permission to harass Saul. God evidently did this as a judgment against Saul; the evil spirit would intensify Saul's paranoid jealousy, abandoning him to his own evil fate. Either he would be repentant or hardened further.

CHARACTERISTICS OF A SPEAR THROWER

Saul, for all his talent and military prowess, exhibited some troubling character flaws that debilitated him from the beginning and doomed him to failure as a spiritual leader. As we move through these you might recognize them as existing in yourself or a church leader you've come to know. Yes, spear throwers are everywhere.

1. He Believed the Kingdom Was His, Not God's

Saul knew that God had given him the kingdom, but once it was his, he acted as if God had no right to take it from him. He did not see himself as serving according to God's good hand, but rather as the kingdom existing for his (Saul's) benefit.

First Samuel records Saul's deliberate disobedience in refusing to kill all of the Amalekites. Oh yes, he claimed he spared the king and the best of the sheep and the oxen to sacrifice to the Lord. But Samuel pointed out: "To obey is better than sacrifice, and to heed is better than the fat of rams" (1 Samuel 15:22b).

The prophet Samuel didn't stop at simply rebuking Saul but added, "You have rejected the word of the LORD, and the LORD has rejected you as king over Israel!" (verse 26). And, to add to the clarity of the message, Samuel went on to say that, "the LORD has torn the kingdom of Israel from you today and has given it to one of your neighbors—to one better than you" (verse 28). And for good measure, Samuel added that God would not change His mind about this.

How should Saul have responded? He should have replied to Samuel, "The kingdom belongs to God and He has the right to take it from me and give it to whomever He wishes." Instead, Saul replied, "I have sinned. But please honor me before the elders of my people and before Israel" (verse 30). Despite the fact that he was rejected by God, he proudly chose to hang on to the kingdom until his knuckles turned white. He would not give up the power and prestige of the kingdom for anything. He hung on to the kingdom for ten long, torturous years!

There are people whom God blesses. He puts them in positions of authority. He gives them vocations, giftedness, talent, and success. And even when they have forfeited their calling, or have passed the time of their usefulness, they turn out to be spear throwers, hurling accusations and hateful sentiments at everyone in their path.

I know well the story of a pastor who had overstayed his welcome in a church. Various disputes arose and a power play erupted between him and the board. The pastor decided to stay to fight it out, to prove that he was right. Yes, the pastor did outlast the board as eventually they all resigned and the congregation went from four hundred to fifty. When all was in shambles, he also left, evidently assuming that someone else would pick up the pieces of a broken ministry. Twenty years later, the church does not exist.

If there is one single reason why good people turn evil, it is because they fail to recognize God's ownership over their kingdom, their vocation, their resources, their abilities, and above all, their lives. Their insistence that they are owners and not stewards leads them to destroy others in order to protect what they perceive as theirs. They derive their sense of significance and value only through power, watching people squirm under their heavy hand. They are threatened by the realization that what they have is from God who can give it and take it as He wills.

Yes, there are times to stay and fight; but there are also times to leave when it is clear that the people of God are being torn asunder and the presence of the leader (perhaps a pastor) is wounding the sheep rather than healing them. But some would rather split the kingdom to protect their own ego than entrust it into the hands of the One to whom it belongs. So they go down the street and begin a new ministry and take as many people as they can with them. They'd be better off suffering wrong and leaving the church than proving they are right by splitting the kingdom.

You don't have to be a leader in the church to fall into this attitude of entitlement. We must remember: God owns our vocation, resources, and abilities. You and I are stewards of all that God has given us. Our sense of significance and value should not come through personal accomplishment or power. God gives us our talents and resources, and He can take them away. Like Job, we should be able to say, "The LORD gave and the LORD has taken away; may the name of the LORD be praised" (Job 1:21).

Who does *your* kingdom belong to?

2. He Displayed Acute Insecurity and Jealousy

Second, Saul was obsessed with insecurity and jealousy. When David and the other men returned from killing Goliath, the women met them saying, "Saul has slain his thousands, and David his tens of thousands" (1 Samuel 18:7). This galled Saul and he eyed David from that time on and asked, "What more can he get but the kingdom?" (verse 8). Saul had no reason to fear David, yet his jealousy made him paranoid and easily threatened by the young man's successes. I see it too often with senior pastors who hire young, talented associates. The moment the young associate gains a following, the trouble starts. Eventually, after dodging so many spears, the associate picks up and makes his exit, wounded and defeated.

There are some people who always have to be the center of attention: "The bride at every wedding . . . and the corpse at every funeral," as a friend of mine puts it! They are threatened by anyone who might make them look bad; they are willing to take credit for what others have done but deny to others the right to succeed. These are people who will magnify the faults of others, but will "not own their own stuff" as the saying goes. In rages of jealousy, they become spear throwers who want to destroy what they perceive to be their competition. Of course, what they do is often out of sight; publicly they are well controlled and kind, but behind the scenes they plot another's downfall.

3. He Displayed a Manipulative and Divisive Spirit

Third, Saul tried to drive a wedge between people. He attempted to manipulate his son, Jonathan, to kill David. It's hard for me to imagine such obsessive jealousy. But spear throwers don't look at life through a clear lens. Thankfully, Jonathan does not obey his father but actually helps David escape. For this the young lad gets a tongue-lashing from his vengeful father. Spear throwers seek to sow discord, believing that if they divide they can conquer. (You can read of Saul's anger against David and then his own son in 1 Samuel 19:1–11a; 20:24–33.)

He will become a whisperer, criticizing one person to another; he will appeal to the ego of the person he is trying to control, as he discredits the person's friends. He will slander anyone who can bring an accusation against him, hoping to destroy the person's reputation so that when the accusation comes, he can dismiss it. In other words, the evil controller wants to make sure that all potential "enemies" are discredited before they can even fight. We must be careful that we do not try to undermine with "whispers" those with whom we disagree.

You might wonder whether Saul had any compassion for David. Early on in the relationship he professed love for David. But as time passed, his conscience was hardened. When a man gives himself to destroy others, he becomes emotionally numb, incapable of empathy. He actually disengages his emotions, so that he has no feeling for those he is hurting. His natural bent of caring is neutralized through rationalization and anger. Emotionally he is, as the saying goes, "zoned out."

Does not the father who abuses his son have sympathy for him as the child cries for mercy? The answer is no, he does not. The truly narcissistic, abusive personality is obsessed with only one thing: that his authority (control) be exercised. Control is his lifeblood; it is in the marrow of his bones; it is his one satisfaction, his one opportunity to show to himself (if not to others) that he really is someone after all. His anger at perceived injustices must be appeased. In his perverted thinking, abusing others is his only way of making this crooked world straight.

4. He Lived by His Own Set of Rules

Spear throwers don't abide by the rules they make for others. Saul in obedience to God's command put out all the witches from Israel. And yet, when he saw the end of his life nearing, in desperation, he went to the witch at Endor to know what to do next. This is called the Law of the Grand Exception—I am not bound by the rules I make for you. Spear throwers play only by their own rules when they want their victim.

The spear thrower believes what he does is right simply by virtue of the fact that he does it. Reasoning with him is a waste of time. Everything you say to him is turned a half turn and comes out twisted. His raging desire for control meets a warped personal need and appears to be insatiable. All of reality is interpreted through his lens—a bent lens to be sure, but a lens nonetheless. He exercises his supposed godhood, protecting his only source of personal identity. He is mad but he thinks he is the only sane man in the kingdom.

Why is it that God chose Saul and let him rule so long? Gene Edwards in his book *A Tale of Three Kings* provides compelling insight into this nagging question.

> Why does God do such a thing? The answer is both simple and shocking. He sometimes gives unworthy

vessels a greater portion of power, so that it might eventually be revealed for all to see the true state of internal nakedness within that man.

Remember: God sometimes gives power to men for unseen reasons. A man can be living in the grossest of sin and the outward gift will be working perfectly.[1]

Edwards contends further that God wants to take out the Saul in us:

Saul is in your bloodstream, in the marrow of your bones. He makes up the very flesh and muscle of your heart. He is mixed into your soul; he inhabits the nuclei of your atoms. King Saul is one with you. You are King Saul.[2]

Edwards believes that the reason God allowed Saul to hang on to the kingdom for ten long years after he was rejected is to take the Saul out of David's heart! David, if unbroken, had the potential of being King Saul number two.

DEFENDING AGAINST A SPEAR THROWER

So what do you do if you live with a spear thrower? Or how should you respond if you encounter one at work—or if a relative turns on you without provocation?

The first thing to do when someone is throwing spears is to *duck*! That may sound a bit tongue-in-cheek, but avoiding the individual is the best strategy. David escaped out of Saul's presence twice. He didn't hang around to become a martyr. He actually escaped, and thus made sure that Saul missed his target.

It's not wrong to get away from a spear thrower if you can. Putting physical and certainly emotional distance between you and the perpetrator is advised. It may mean changing jobs or moving to a different neighborhood. It might mean putting boundaries in place if the individual is an in-law or other relative. It's the strategy the young associate pastor I wrote about at the beginning of the chapter employed. Once he realized the odds were stacked against him, he left without a word, never to return again. He grew weary of the spears shot in his direction, so he chose to get out of the vicinity of the subtly enraged senior pastor.

Of course, if you are living with an abusive husband, go for help! Especially move quickly if the abuse involves your children. Whether it's fathers who molest or abuse their children, or mothers bent on destroying the other members of the family through guilt, manipulation, and deceit, there is a time for boundaries. You must seek help for dealing with those whose behavior is toxic.

Saul's false humility kept David off balance, for there were times when Saul could be charming and appear to be very accommodating. Five times he promised to mend his ways, saying that he was repenting. No doubt this gave David hope, thinking that the king's attitude was changing for the better, perhaps permanently. Just as a control freak might repent and offer hope of reform, so Saul sent mixed signals. But eventually he would change his mind about having changed his mind. His repentance was never deep enough, because he refused to see himself in the presence of God.

Never take what a spear thrower says too personally. You have to understand that spear throwers see the evil in their hearts as belonging to others. The hostility and anger that you receive from them unjustifiably are very likely accusations that apply to them. That's why it's important you not take their words to heart. Their words and actions cast judgment on themselves. Unfortunately, that's what happens when individuals with weak character end up in places of influence or positions of power. They are so flawed and paranoid that everyone around them becomes a victim.

A friend gave me this bit of advice. "Never wrestle with a pig. For one thing you will become dirty; second, the pig will love it; and third, he plays by a different set of rules." How true! Spear throwers are essentially irrational people. They are not bound by fairness, truthfulness, decency, or respect. You can't reason with them, you can't meet them on a level playing field. I've seen spear throwers connect dots that are unrelated, make wild charges, and categorize everyone as either evil or good (good meaning those who agree with him). There is no rational negotiation that would enable you to meet them halfway. Either you agree with them and thereby come under their control or you will be cast aside, branded by their own twisted view of reality. Solomon wrote, "When the wicked rise to power, people go into hiding" (Proverbs 28:28).

Second, don't become a spear thrower yourself! We have to commend David for not wrenching the spear out of the wall and throwing it back at Saul. I would have probably taken the spear and said, "Just watch this, Saul; now it's my turn!" How often we can use our imagination to visualize ourselves throwing a spear at our enemy and how good it would feel to hit our target. But retaliation is not a healthy strategy.

David passed on two chances to assassinate Saul. In both instances, Saul was in pursuit of David, hoping to kill him. David was living in caves among the rocks near En Gedi, a barren stretch of the Judean desert. When David and his men found Saul sleeping in a caves, David's men insisted that they be given permission to kill the wicked king. But instead of seeking revenge, David came along and cut off part of his cloak. David's men thought him crazy for not killing the insane Saul, but David said, "The LORD forbid that I should do such a thing to . . . the LORD's anointed, or lift my hand against him; for he is the anointed of the LORD" (1 Samuel 24:6).

David was willing to let God take care of his enemy. Jesus said, "Do not render evil for evil." But keep in mind that the Bible teaches clearly that ultimately spear throwers are under God's sovereign control. A two-year-old child in a stroller was rapidly turning his little steering wheel to the right, but he was going to the left, nonetheless. His direction was not determined by him, but by his mother; his steering wheel was not connected to anything that mattered. Just so the wicked: They have the illusion of control, but their fate is in God's hands. How quickly their world can disintegrate; how quickly their lives can be brought to an end. While they do their evil deeds, we believe that God takes up the cause of the oppressed. We don't need to throw spears if we trust in God.

Finally, look for God's purpose in the difficult ordeal. God certainly could have taken Saul out of the picture long before

He did and spared David the agony of the desert. But God's purpose for David included the desert experience—God needed David to learn patience, humility, and absolute surrender before he was fit to rule. How better to train the young shepherd king than in the school of adversity and injustice. Saul was the anvil on which God forged true kingly character in David.

IS THERE A SPEAR THROWER IN YOU?

Do you realize and believe some of King Saul may be within you? Whether you are a man or woman reading this, part of King Saul probably is within. How much? Here are some questions that will help you find out the extent to which you have Saul's heart.

- Am I envious of those who have more influence and resources?
- How would I react if in my service in the church (e.g., teaching Sunday school, playing an instrument, being a greeter, usher, or assisting in the kitchen) someone asked me to step down from this ministry?
- Do I ever wish someone would "get his" for something he did or said against me—or a friend of mine?
- Do I let people know about an injustice done to me, hoping for sympathy and/or trying to make the other person look bad?

Yes, as Edwards says, God wanted to make sure David's heart had been emptied of the potential of becoming another Saul! David had it within him to become a spear thrower. He had it within him to do what his own son Absalom did, to split the kingdom in a rebellious fit. All of those seeds were in David's heart. And they reside in your heart and mine too.

It is my firm conviction that there are some people God wants simply to live in pain in order to bring about genuine brokenness. Paul wrote in 2 Corinthians 4:7–9 that "we have this treasure in jars of clay to show that this all-surpassing power is from God and not from us. We are hard pressed on every side, but not crushed; perplexed, but not in despair; persecuted, but not abandoned; struck down, but not destroyed." So what would be the purpose of all that trouble? It's a process that *ensures* godliness and dependence on the Lord, not on ourselves. Someone has wisely said that *the work that God does in us when we wait is usually more important than the thing for which we wait!*

We must come to the point in our lives when we realize that a blessing might be entailed in our hurt. Think of the deep work God does in our hearts when we have to do what is most difficult—forgive those who do not deserve forgiveness. But in the process, we become godly. I've had to conclude that God would not allow spear throwers into my life if He did not intend that their arrows bear fruit in my life.

Once I was having breakfast with a friend who had married a spear thrower. She was exceedingly critical of him— vicious at times, even in public. I remember thinking to myself, *I don't think I could endure such suffering.*

When I confessed my thoughts to my friend, he startled

me with his response. He said, "You know that all of my life I've been a very impatient person. I couldn't listen to people who had problems in their marriages or with their children. Now I have a listening ear because I have a broken heart." Only pain will do that for you—soften you and make you a more useful individual to the Lord. For some people the pain is difficult circumstances or a chronic illness or tragedy. For other people . . . it is people—impossible, obnoxious people, such as manipulative, overbearing, or too involved in-laws.

Finally, wait for the Lord and trust Him to use you in your struggles. David lived in solitude as a fugitive—anointed as king of Israel—but stuck in a holding pattern in the Judean wilderness. Yet from the barrenness of those desert years flowed the life-giving streams of the Psalms. Can you imagine your Christian experience without the refrains of David's psalms? Here is only a sampling of this rich treasure of comfort and strength that he wrote while on the run:

> I sought the LORD, and he answered me; he delivered me from all my fears . . . this poor man called, and the LORD heard him; he saved him out of all his troubles. (Psalm 34:4, 6)

> Trust in the LORD and do good; dwell in the land and enjoy safe pasture. Delight yourself in the LORD and he will give you the desires of your heart. (Psalm 37:3–4)

> I waited patiently for the LORD; he turned to me and heard my cry. He lifted me out of the slimy pit, out of

the mud and mire; he set my feet on a rock and gave me
a firm place to stand. (Psalm 40:1–2)

This desert king wrote more than a dozen psalms during
that period of time and spoke peace and comfort and confidence to generations.

I remember going through a difficult time in my own life.
There was pain in my heart because of a spear thrower. I recall
taking time each day to read through the Psalms, five or six
each day. Every time I saw new insights. Every time I would
look into the life of David, and I would be encouraged.

How could David have written what he did unless God
had put a Saul over him with a spear pointed in his direction?
David's suffering became my source of encouragement.

Jesus had the power to control all the events of His life, yet
He exercised none of it. When a crowd gathered to arrest Him,
He made an astounding statement: "This hour and the power
of darkness are yours" (see Luke 22:53). In effect He said,
"Today, you win; today you get to control the outcome of
events. Go ahead, nail Me to the cross."

This crowd of evil controllers went ahead with their diabol-
ical deed, and as a result Christ purchased our redemption.
Those in the crowd were responsible, yes; but God would use
these control freaks to accomplish His own purposes. Jesus
teaches us this: Because I believe my Father is in control, I
don't have to be.

You can't reconcile with a spear thrower, but they have
much to teach us about ourselves and our God. I close this
chapter with excerpts from Psalm 37, written by David in a

time when he needed to be encouraged about the ultimate fate of his enemies—and a prayer we can use when facing those armed with spears:

A PRAYER WHEN FACING THOSE WITH SPEARS

Father, we pray that we will not fret because of evil men or be envious of those who do wrong; for like the grass they will soon wither, like the green plants they will soon die away. . . . Help us to be still before the Lord and wait patiently for Him; let us not fret when men succeed in their ways, when they carry out their wicked schemes. May we refrain from anger and turn from wrath. . . . For evil men will be cut off, but those who hope in the Lord will inherit the land. . . . The Lord laughs at the wicked, for He knows their day is coming.

Grant us faith to believe what we have prayed, in Jesus' name. Amen.

CHRISTIANS IN THE COURTROOM

"MY DAD TRUSTED MY BROTHER to be the executor of his will because my brother is an attorney," began a letter sent by a radio listener I'll call Michael. "My dad told me he was leaving about $300,000. My brother says that I am going to get about $10,000 or $20,000, because he says everything else is fees and taxes, and all the rest. When I want to see the books, he's so defensive."

Reading on, I realized Michael's dilemma: "My wife has cancer, and I don't have money to send my kids to college; we're in desperate straits. I know right well my dad intended that I should get my fair share. What should I do? I want to sue him."

Michael is a Christian. And his brother claims to be one too.

Another man told me that he owed a Christian organization $300,000. He was not disputing that fact. But his business had gone belly-up, and he got into some serious financial trouble. He was trying to figure out how he could pay off his debt, trying to work something out, when suddenly he was served with papers and a lawsuit was in progress.

Two years later he told me, "Up till now I have spent $250,000 in legal fees. They have spent about $250,000 in legal fees." That's half a million dollars. Let's remember that the dispute was over $300,000. But some people are so consumed with destroying others that they are willing to end up with less money, if only they can make sure that their perceived enemy gets his "just deserts." Now, these folks are Christians, or at least that's what they say.

Then there's that celebrated story from the news about a woman who was disciplined by her church for adultery. She was not denying the adultery. But instead of humbling herself, accepting responsibility, and complying with the terms of church discipline, she decided to sue the church for an abuse of her civil rights.

Our obsession with individual rights and a litigious society have joined forces to make suing one another standard fare. That woman felt right at home admitting her adultery yet protested through a court of law the discipline of the church of which she was a member.

COURT TV RIGHT IN YOUR LIVING ROOM

Why is America such a litigious nation? There's a rather simplistic answer with more complicated implications. We are living in a culture that exalts individual rights even as it accepts a decline (and corruption) of personal morals and integrity. Put the two together and you have a recipe for incredible lawsuits.

Remember the news account—yes, it's a true story—of two sets of parents who went to court after their children, playing in a sandbox, got into a big argument? It used to be that parents could work those things out, when character was important. But today without character they cannot even settle such minor matters. Today we need a law for everything, and God help us if we don't get what we believe to be our individual "rights."

My wife and I traveled to Switzerland a few years ago. We took a chairlift to the top of a mountain and walked around up there for a couple of miles. The scenery was breathtaking. Along the way, about fifteen feet from the path, we noticed a fence with just two wires. It was the kind of fence that any small child could crawl through. Yet beyond that fence was a sheer cliff that dropped several hundred feet into an abyss.

In America, if a child crossed that fence and fell to his death, we would look quickly for the most vulnerable person to sue. In Switzerland, if a child is killed because of falling through the fence, the responsibility falls squarely on the parents and it stands as a tragic accident. What a difference in attitude and responsibility!

America has seen an alarming decrease in individual responsibility and a heightened increase in personal rights in the last fifty to sixty years. And unfortunately, God's Word notwithstanding, Christians have absorbed the culture and are suing one another.

The Bible clearly outlines the involvement of Christians in the courtroom. As we will see, when we seek our own justice when personal injury occurs, we ignore God's ability to obtain eventual justice and our need to forgive. To better understand our response and God's, as Michael sought after his lawyer brother had apparently withheld part of his inheritance, we need to look at what the Bible says about legal action among and by believers after an offense.

AVOIDING LAWSUITS: A BIBLICAL PERSPECTIVE

The apostle Paul specifically addressed this issue of disputes in 1 Corinthians 6. Apparently, some Christians were falling prey to shortsightedness and suing each other in courts of law. And in this passage Paul provides several excellent reasons why believers should avoid pursuing fellow believers in civil court. Take a close look at the passage.

> If any of you has a dispute with another, dare he take it before the ungodly for judgment instead of before the saints? Do you not know that the saints will judge the world? And if you are to judge the world, are you not competent to judge trivial cases? Do you not know that we will judge angels? How much more the things of this life! Therefore, if you have disputes about such matters, appoint as judges even men of little account in the church! I say this to shame you. Is it possible that there is nobody among you wise enough to judge

a dispute between believers? But instead, one brother goes to law against another—and this in front of unbelievers! The very fact that you have lawsuits among you means you have been completely defeated already. Why not rather be wronged? Why not rather be cheated? Instead, you yourselves cheat and do wrong, and you do this to your brothers. (1 Corinthians 6:1–8)

Paul outlines clear advice on the reasons believers should avoid going to court against one another. They are compelling and ring strikingly true in this age of rampant litigation.

1. Our Witness to the World

As Christians we avoid civil suits against fellow Christians because of our witness to the world. By suing one another we openly display to the world that our faith in Christ makes no difference when it comes to settling personal disputes. Try as they might, the people of the world can't see any difference between themselves and us. We demand our rights just as the world does, and in case you don't realize it, Christians can also be just as nasty in court as the people of the world.

For us, Christ should make all the difference in settling personal disputes. Unbelievers are always trying to find evidence to prove that those who profess to know Christ are no different from those who don't. Christians suing Christians is a compelling piece of evidence that our faith system is lacking—especially if we have to rely on secular wisdom to manage our human affairs.

2. A Rejection of Secular Values

Second, Paul is concerned about a Christian's unhealthy acceptance of worldly values. Jesus commanded His disciples to be in the world but not *of* the world. Being *in* the world is strategic—allowing for the light of Christ to shine into darkness. Being *of* the world is capitulation to the world's system of values and leads to an ineffective witness. The light is snuffed out.

Paul asked, "Do you not know that the saints will judge the world?" Then he adds this further detail: "Do you not know that we will judge angels?" Perhaps this is a reference to fallen angels, which means that Christians might have a hand in judging the Devil and his demons. Or if it refers to the good angels, it could simply mean that we will be above angels in rank and authority. At any rate, Paul says that since we will one day sit in judgment of other beings, how is it that we do not have enough wisdom to settle personal disputes? We are to renounce the values of this world now, as we ready for our service in heaven. With an eternal perspective, we recognize the truth of the matter: Such cases are trivial and inconsequential compared to matters of judging the demons and ruling over angels in the world to come.

Catch your breath before you read what Jesus said in Revelation 3:21: "To him who overcomes, I will give the right to sit with me on my throne, just as I overcame and sat down with my Father on his throne." That's a remarkable statement! Jesus said, "You are going to sit on the throne with Me in the coming kingdom, judging the world, judging angels," so the implication is that surely we can judge the matters which divide us on earth.

Paul is reminding believers to keep an eternal perspective. Judging angels and demons cannot in any measure compare to what's involved in settling petty differences. Maybe you've been cheated out of money. Now you expect the whole world to stop on its axis because somebody did something to you that was hurtful and wrong. The Bible says that's a worldly attitude and a trivial pursuit.

3. Respect for the Authority of the Church

The Christian life is a life of submission. We submit to Christ, we submit to our mates, we submit to one another in love, and we submit to the authority of the body of Christ. That's God's plan. By going to court against a fellow believer we show a blatant disregard for God's plan for orderly living and righteousness. Paul says in effect, "Are there not wise people in your church who are willing to arbitrate? Can't you be submissive? If there are two brothers and they are in the same church, couldn't you take this to an elder or a wise person in the church who would be able to arbitrate between the two of you, and you would accept the verdict?"

The answer is too often *no*. Few Christians are willing to submit to one another when it comes to settling personal disputes, especially in regard to money or family issues. Instead, when judgments don't go our way, we simply get mad and leave. You can always attend some other church and refuse submission for the glory of God. What a sad way to live in light of the tremendous resources available to you in Christ.

Believe me, elders and other leaders in the church are not infallible. They do make mistakes. But mature Christians live such submitted lives that in spite of those human shortfalls, they trust God's eternal plan.

"But I have to right the wrong!" That's the argument some Christians use to get around Paul's clear teaching. Paul anticipated that and said, "Why not rather be wronged? Why not rather be cheated? Instead, you yourselves cheat and do wrong, and you do this to your brothers" (1 Corinthians 6:7–8). The wise apostle pointed out that the mere presence of such civil disputes among Christians shows a defeated faith. Yes, to suffer wrong would glorify God more than going to court to set matters straight. Paul's question is penetrating for us to consider.

A Christian attorney I know reports that in all the cases that he has seen, when a Christian goes to court with another Christian, he never receives blessing even if he wins the case. For the Christian, winning a judgment against a fellow believer comes at an enormous price—the loss of a brother or sister in the Lord, a diminished witness, and a weakened church body.

PUTTING IT INTO PRACTICE

In relationships among believers, every means, short of a lawsuit, should be pursued in trying to resolve a conflict. Paul's point is clear: In matters of personal injury or loss, we should be willing to suffer wrong, believing that God keeps the books and He will adjudicate the matter, if not in this life, then in the life to come. This is proof of our trust that the Judge of all the earth will do right.

Of course, when a crime has been committed and the state has a compelling interest to intervene, Christians should co-operate with the authorities, whether the offender is a Christian or non-Christian. There might also be instances in which we ourselves have not been injured, but we take legal action to protect the rights of others. In such instances where the situation is unclear, we must seek godly advice from church leaders.

Should a Christian ever sue an employer or hospital? The late Larry Burkett wrote that "corporations and businesses are entities controlled or solely owned by persons, but they appear to have no rights under biblical guidelines, except by prevailing law. So, it's not unbiblical for Christians to sue corporations in order to require them to meet their legal obligations." He went on to say that if a Christian sues a hospital, it should only be for hospital costs, rehabilitation, compensation, etc. "However, suing for damages in order to punish the hospital or physician should never be pursued."[1] Clearly, no Christian should ever seek revenge (Deuteronomy 32:35; Romans 12:17–20).

Burkett also cautioned that even if we think we have the "right to sue," that does not mean that we should exercise that right. He concluded with this question: "Finally, if we really believe that everything belongs to God, the question remains, 'Do I trust God or do I just say that I trust God?'"[2]

Of course, we have every right to defend ourselves when someone brings a lawsuit against us, even as Paul defended himself against unjust accusations. When falsely arrested or mistreated, he appealed to Roman law to gain his freedom and to affirm his rights (Acts 16:35–37; 22:25; 25:11). Yet, even here, the Christian views things differently: Justice denied on earth earns great rewards in heaven if endured for the sake of Christ. (See James 5:1–9 and 1 Peter 3: 14–16.)

In cases of personal injury or loss among believers, though, resolution outside the courtroom is preferred.

Thankfully, there are several organizations today that provide Christian mediation for those who are willing to submit themselves to it. We can be grateful that some have seen the need to provide both wise legal and spiritual input into disputes among Christians.[3]

THE PRIVILEGE OF SUFFERING WRONG

Keep in mind that the 1 Corinthians 6 passage is saying that it is far better for you to suffer wrong and be defrauded than to initiate a lawsuit in a secular court against another believer. Of course, we all struggle with suffering wrong, but that is the Christian path. When called to suffer wrongfully, our natural instinct is not to give thanks to God for it, but we should. God is watching carefully and notes our response. Here are several reasons why we should be willing to suffer wrong.

First, when we suffer an injustice from a fellow believer we follow the path of Jesus. Paul wrote to the Philippians:

Your attitude should be the same as that of Christ Jesus: Who, being in very nature God, did not consider equality with God something to be grasped, but made himself nothing, taking the very nature of a servant, being made in human likeness. And being found in appearance as a man, he humbled himself and became obedient to death—even death on a cross! (Philippians 2:5-8)

There was no greater wrong suffered unjustly than the death of Christ. He suffered at the hands of His own people—an injustice so foul and heinous that anyone would have supported His retaliation and defense. Yet, He submitted to it for a higher purpose—the glory of God. When you resign your rights and submit to God's plan, you align yourself with the spirit of Jesus—the spirit of humble submission and suffering.

Second, suffering a wrong gives God an opportunity to display His grace. In fact, all suffering gives God an opportunity to display more grace in our lives. But there is no suffering that is as painful, in my opinion, as the suffering of injustice. Being afflicted with cancer or some other disease can be an agonizing ordeal to be sure. But there's no one trying to get even with you, or slandering you, or stabbing you in the back. Cancer hurts the body; injustice oppresses the soul. The desire for revenge is strong, especially when there is no hope of seeing the score evened in this life. But in those desperate moments God says, "My grace is sufficient."

Grace upon grace, like an elastic band, stretches to the extent of your need. Injustice has a way of cutting us deeply. But in the middle of the cut, God comes along with healing salve and gives us grace and strength to endure.

IT'S OK TO SUFFER WRONG

Suffering injustice does hurt. When someone tries to get even with you, or slanders you, or betrays you, the injustice of it can oppress your soul. Yet the Bible clearly says we can and should bear under such suffering, for three right reasons:

1. We are following the path of Jesus. He went all the way to the cross to suffer wrong. Submit to God's plan and you align yourself with the spirit of Jesus—the spirit of humble submission.
2. We give God an opportunity to display His grace in our lives. And God promises that His grace is sufficient for every affliction (2 Corinthians 12:9).
3. We can display our hope in another world. We rest in the assurance that justice deferred one day will be justice served—when Jesus, the Righteous Judge, returns to rule.

Finally, suffering a wrong provides an opportunity to demonstrate your hope in another world. Consider Paul's words of hope to the Thessalonian believers, suffering injustice because of their faith:

Therefore, among God's churches we boast about your perseverance and faith in all the persecutions and trials you are enduring. All this is evidence that God's judgment is right, and as a result you will be counted worthy of the kingdom of God, for which you are suffering. God is just: He will pay back trouble to those who trouble you and give relief to you who are troubled, and to us as well. This will happen when the Lord Jesus is revealed from heaven in blazing fire with his powerful angels. (2 Thessalonians 1:4–7)

Justice will be served when Jesus returns. This world is not all there is. For the believer, justice is deferred. When the Righteous Judge of the universe returns, He will deliver His final judgments on behalf of the righteous.

I am not suggesting Christians give up their desire and aggressive pursuit of justice on behalf of the helpless. Such convictions serve us well as we carry the message of Christ to the nations. In fact, that desire for justice is built into our lives as image-bearers of God. However, I am saying that we do not have to right every wrong; we do not have to see justice in this life in order to believe we shall see it in the life to come. We must leave many matters to the Supreme Court of the universe—to be judged by the Chief Justice, Jesus Christ. There is a day coming when every single wrong will be answered.

In these unresolved conflicts God often gives extraordinary grace. I received a letter from a man who wrote in part, "My angry, estranged wife served me papers intended to sue me for all I owned. I knew that she had an unscrupulous attorney who would not stop at anything to destroy me. So, rather than fight, I chose to give her the $300,000 she asked for—virtually all we ever had. At the age of fifty-five, I had to start over, also taking care of the two children she did not want. But God gave me grace in my poverty and in my work. Eventually, I was able to earn a decent living, and we will survive. What surprised me the most was the grace God gave to me to not be bitter but to accept this as a trial from *His* hand, and not from the hand of someone who hates me."

Amazing! But his response acknowledges that God provides now and one day will fully reward those who obey Him.

THE JUDGMENT SEAT OF CHRIST

Let me describe an all-too-common scenario: A couple chooses to walk hand in hand through life, so they marry and eventually have children, but the man runs off and abandons his family while he lives a life of luxury with another woman, without ever paying child support payments. Supposedly he's a Christian, yet not acting like one. The man eventually dies and so does the wife he so cruelly wronged. Both arrive in heaven. What happens next? Does God smile and allow them to walk hand in hand into their new eternal state, acting as if nothing happened? After all, they're both Christians. Both are covered in the righteousness of Christ.

That's not the way it's going to be. That's why the Bible says, "So we make it our goal to please him, whether we are at home in the body or away from it. For we must all appear before the judgment seat of Christ, that each one may receive what is due him for the things done while in the body, whether good or bad" (2 Corinthians 5:9–10). Yes, that is a reference to Christians giving an account for how they lived here on earth.

It is true that Christians are welcomed into heaven on the basis of Christ's perfect righteousness, but it is also true that we face a rather thorough review of our lives to give account for the way we have lived. Justice will be meted out in that final verdict. The penalty will not be separation from God—but perfect justice will be displayed for all to see.

Will we as Christians see our sins at the judgment seat? If we do, they will be represented to us as being forgiven, but in some way God will make a thorough evaluation. And it might well be that those who lived with selfish, worldly values will find that their role in the kingdom is diminished. That's why Paul says to Christians, "Do not take revenge, my friends, but leave room for God's wrath, for it is written: 'It is mine to avenge; I will repay,' says the Lord" (Romans 12:19).

And in the case of the unsaved, they will face the full brunt of their evil for all of eternity, as their life is dragged out in the presence of God. The great white throne judgment at which the unconverted of all the ages will be judged, will be according to truth. People will be judged on the basis of what they did with what they knew. And justice will be accurately balanced (Revelation 20:11–15). That's why we will sing for all of eternity, "Just and true are your ways, O King of Saints."

I urge you to give to the Lord that terrible desire to get even with the one who has wronged you. Someday, the innocent will be vindicated and the exploiters will be exposed. That brother who lied about his dad's will—he will have to answer to God. The mother-in-law who relentlessly meddled in her daughter's life—she will have to give an account. The woman who wrongly accused you of having an affair—she will stand before God for her deeds. Can you trust the Lord with all of that? It will be better to suffer the wrong and trust God's justice to prevail than to live with the pain of bitterness. Remember it is possible for you to be right about a matter and still let it go . . . earth is not the final arbiter of right and wrong.

Let us take our vengeance, and like a pitcher of water, pour it out at the foot of the cross. There we received endless and repeated pardon, and let us now extend it to others.

A PRAYER FOR GOD'S JUSTICE

Father, grant us the faith to believe that You are the judge of both the righteous and the unrighteous. Grant us the gift of peace, knowing that justice is in Your hands. We pray that as believers we will obey Your Word and have the courage to suffer wrong rather than to take a brother or sister to court. Give us wise people in our churches to help us settle disputes so that our witness to the world might be clear and strong.

We give You our emotions and hopes for the future. Let us look to You in faith and thanksgiving for the justice that our hearts seek. In Jesus' name. Amen.

FROM BITTERNESS TO BLESSING

AS A FARM BOY GROWING UP, one of my chores was to weed the garden. I absolutely hated it. I had to put a stake in the ground to distinguish between what was weeded and what still needed to be weeded because I did the task so poorly! But in the process I learned something valuable. There are essentially two ways to take care of weeds: Cut them off at ground level or dig them out at the roots. Only the second solves the problem.

When bitterness takes root in your life, it's nearly impossible to deal with it at the surface level. I've learned that our choice to forgive might begin at a superficial level, but it must continue to go deeper. At first the feelings of anger and pain might go dormant for hours or days, but eventually, the bitterness raises its ugly head. We need to attack bitterness at its root. That's what this chapter is about—root-level forgiveness and whenever possible, root-level reconciliation.

BITTERNESS OVERFLOWING

In Hebrews we read, "See to it that no one misses the grace of God and that no bitter root grows up to cause trouble and defile many" (12:15). This verse teaches us two things about bitterness: First, it has a root; and second, as the root spreads, it defiles many.

The impact of bitterness is not merely on the individual harboring it; bitterness also overflows. The bitter soul always attempts to build alliances—to recruit individuals to affirm his pain and plight. That's one way bitterness overflows. Another way is through angry living. Bitterness takes hold of a father, for example, and he becomes passive-aggressive in his behavior toward his children and mate. One day he's father of the year—gentle, loving, affirming, and gracious—the next day he erupts like Mount Vesuvius, spilling his lavalike bitterness and rancor on everyone in his path. The impact, like carefully arranged dominoes, wounds the children and the marriage. One bitter man or woman can infect the whole community and bring it down in flames. There's no such thing as a bitter person who keeps the bitterness to himself.

Thankfully, there's hope for rooting out the insidious threat. The Bible shows us how one remarkable man, by allowing God to heal his pain, impacted the spiritual legacy of an entire generation. His name was Joseph—a man of total forgiveness.

JOSEPH THE DREAMER

Joseph was only seventeen when the biblical story picks up. He had few strikes against him. He was the second youngest of twelve brothers. He was talented and handsome. And he happened to be his father's favorite son. That alone put him on a collision course with his older brothers. Joseph's father, Jacob, had given him a richly ornamented robe, which in effect said, "I want you to have the blessing of the firstborn." That ended up being a serious misjudgment on Jacob's part, with eleven other sons looking on who were by nature angry and opinionated.

Joseph was also a dreamer—not of daydreams, but of literal dreams. He saw visions in his sleep and they turned out to be from the Lord. Each dream revealed another sequence of events that would lead to his exaltation over his brothers. The more he dreamed, the more it became clear the Lord had great plans for him. Not surprisingly, his destiny was impossible for his jealous brothers to embrace, and "they hated him all the more." The story is in Genesis 37:

> Joseph had a dream, and when he told it to his brothers, they hated him all the more. He said to them, "Listen to this dream I had: We were binding sheaves of grain out in the field when suddenly my sheaf rose and stood upright, while your sheaves gathered around mine and bowed down to it."
>
> His brothers said to him, "Do you intend to reign over us? Will you actually rule us?" And they hated him all the more because of his dream and what he had said. (Genesis 37:5–8)

And that is how, at the young age of seventeen, Joseph's journey into suffering began. Later Joseph revealed yet another dream: "I had another dream, and this time the sun and moon and eleven stars were bowing down to me" (verse 9). Hearing this, his brothers threw back their heads and howled in jealousy. When Joseph told his father, Jacob gave a stinging rebuke (verses 10–11). Nothing good would come of any of it.

REASONS FOR BITTERNESS

One day Jacob sent young Joseph out to check on the welfare of his older brothers who were tending the family sheep in the hill country. When they saw him coming along, they devised a plot to kill him. They said, in effect, "Let's kill him and then see what becomes of his dreams!" (Genesis 37:17–19).

Do you know anyone who would like to end your dream? A missionary told me, "Nothing would gladden the heart of a coworker more than if I were to fail." So one man's dream is to put an end to someone else's dream! Jealousy, envy, and territorialism always plot the downfall of others. That's what was going on here.

Betrayed by Brothers

Fortunately for Joseph, one of his brothers, Reuben, intervened and dissuaded the others from taking Joseph's life. Instead they threw the teenage boy into a pit and left him to die alone. They then sat down for their midday meal. While eating, they spotted a nearby caravan of Ishmaelite traders. Then another of the brothers had a plan that would fully spare Joseph's life, although it would bring great loss to their father:

Judah said to his brothers, "What will we gain if we kill our brother and cover up his blood? Come, let's sell him to the Ishmaelites and not lay hands on him; after all, he is our brother, our own flesh and blood." His brothers agreed. So when the Midianite merchants came by, his brothers pulled Joseph up out of the cistern and sold him for twenty shekels of silver to the Ishmaelites, who took him to Egypt. (Genesis 37:26–28)

As far as his brothers were concerned, that was the end of their pesky brother. They dipped Joseph's coat in the blood of a slain wild animal and presented it to Jacob. They told Jacob they found the coat on the road, tricking him into believing Joseph had been killed and eaten. Jacob mourned for Joseph for over twenty years, while his deceitful older sons managed to keep their heinous secret. The older brothers completely forgot Joseph.

I had a clock that beeped every hour. I could not get the thing to stop beeping. I didn't want to simply toss it, so I left it in my study. Every hour on the hour it beeped. This went on for weeks until finally the battery died. The beeping stopped. That's precisely what happens to your conscience in concealing sin. The conscience keeps beeping but finally it dies and no longer affects you. The brothers hardened their hearts and kept the lie to themselves.

As for Joseph, his fate, humanly speaking, was worse than death. To be a slave in Egypt was doubly terrifying for a stranger who didn't know the language or the culture. He could expect to work under the most cruel conditions or to be beaten to death. The day he left on the caravan, all hope must have died in his soul. To make matters worse, he knew his brothers were happy about his terrible fate. Their hatred and betrayal stung.

Accused Falsely

There was another good reason for Joseph to be bitter. He was falsely accused and thrown into a dungeon. The story is worth retelling.

He arrived in Egypt and as a slave, he rose to prominence, having found favor in the sight of Potiphar, who was the head of Pharaoh's Secret Service detail. And the Scripture says, "The LORD was with him and . . . gave him success in everything he did" (Genesis 39:3). As a result, he became a trusted advisor in Potiphar's house. A remarkable turn of events. But he had also caught the eye of his boss's wife.

Everything was going well, perhaps too well, actually. Joseph had found favor with God and with Potiphar, who trusted him to take care of all of his household, which included servants and business affairs. Humanly the exaltation was more than Joseph could possibly have expected; clearly God was in all of this for this is not how Joseph had thought it would be. It was almost too good to be true. Enter Potiphar's wife.

Now Joseph was well-built and handsome, and after a while his master's wife took notice of Joseph and said, "Come to bed with me!"

But he refused. "With me in charge," he told her, "my master does not concern himself with anything in the house; everything he owns he has entrusted to my care. (39:6–8)

There were two gifts God had given Joseph that would play a role in his destiny. He was unusually handsome and he possessed a remarkable character. Nevertheless, he ended up the victim of another cruel injustice, this time in the form of a false accusation.

Potiphar's wife was sexually attracted to him. We read, "And though she spoke to Joseph day after day, he refused to go to bed with her or even be with her" (verse 10). The temptation was persistent and in this faraway country, he might have thought that his family would never know. Put two beautiful people together in close environment, and, as Luther said, it is like putting straw on fire and expecting it not to burn! Undoubtedly, Joseph was sorely tempted. Yet, Joseph refused to give in. What followed is surprising, but very believable.

> One day he went into the house to attend to his duties, and none of the household servants was inside. She caught him by his cloak and said, "Come to bed with me!" But he left his cloak in her hand and ran out of the house.
>
> When she saw that he had left his cloak in her hand and had run out of the house, she called her household servants. "Look," she said to them, "this Hebrew has been brought to us to make sport of us! He came in here to sleep with me, but I screamed. When he heard me scream for help, he left his cloak beside me and ran out of the house (verses 11–15).

Imagine the injustice of such an accusation! When Potiphar came home and heard the story, in anger he threw Joseph, his trusted servant, into prison. By now, Joseph had been rejected by his brothers, separated from his beloved father, physically abused (the brothers tore his robe and tossed him into a pit), sold as a slave, and finally imprisoned with shackles for a crime he did not commit. Why? Because he was a gifted, good-looking, amazingly talented young man, who feared God and had a heart of integrity. It just doesn't seem right, does it?

So often we hear, "Do what is right and everything will turn out well." That, of course, is not true, at least not in the short term. Sometimes the cruelest injustices come to those who do what is right. The rewards of obedience are often postponed.

Betrayed by a Friend

While in prison, Joseph met two servants of the pharaoh, one the cupbearer, the other the chief baker of the king. They became his friends, and Joseph willingly interpreted their dreams. The baker's dream revealed his execution. But the cupbearer's dream revealed his release from prison and re-instatement to his place as cupbearer to Pharaoh. After Joseph interpreted his dream he asked his friend to remember him before Pharaoh upon his release—to appeal to him for the injustice of his plight (Genesis 40:8–18). Everything happened according to how Joseph had interpreted it. On the occasion of Pharaoh's birthday, the king restored the cupbearer and hanged the baker. But this chapter in Joseph's life closed as sadly as it had begun—for the chief cupbearer, his friend and the one to whom Joseph had entrusted his whole future, "did not remember Joseph; he forgot him" (40:23).

In prison Joseph had to die three deaths: He had already died to his family; now wrongly accused he had to die to his reputation, and in the end he had to die to his only friend! I'm sure that his dreams died that day when he had every reason to believe that he would be in prison for the rest of his life. He had nothing to look forward to except abuse, monotony, and deprivation.

Psalm 105 provides a very interesting commentary on Joseph's plight as a slave and a prisoner in Egypt. Read what he endured and why:

> [The Lord] called down famine on the land and destroyed all their supplies of food; and he sent a man before them—Joseph, sold as a slave. They bruised his feet with shackles, his neck was put in irons, till what he foretold came to pass, till the word of the LORD proved him true. (Psalm 105:16–19)

All this happened "till the word of the LORD proved him true"! Joseph knew that what he was experiencing was by the divine will and purpose of God. He had every reason to be bitter —to allow his painful circumstances to make him angry and hopeless the rest of his days. Yet, he did not respond that way.

How is that possible? How is it possible for someone with such obvious and valid reasons for bitterness and vengeance to become for us the model of forgiveness and healing? The key is in his response. I want to suggest Joseph responded in five unique ways, which allowed God's healing power and grace to remove the bitterness and pain of his past.

FIVE REMARKABLE RESPONSES TO SUFFERING WRONG

In the previous chapter we considered the privilege of suffering wrong and looked at three reasons to accept suffering. Joseph now shows five right responses when one suffers wrong. They show us how in suffering we may still honor our Lord and even bless others. Here are the five right responses we need to have toward injustice.

1. Choose to Live in the Future and Not in the Past

In Genesis 41, Joseph is released from prison. He was given a position of responsibility back in Pharaoh's government and he married a beautiful young princess, Asenath. Eventually, he fathered two sons. The names given to them give us a clue as to his attitude.

> Before the years of famine came, two sons were born to Joseph by Asenath daughter of Potiphera, priest of On. Joseph named his firstborn Manasseh and said, "It is because God has made me forget all my trouble and all my father's household." The second son he named Ephraim and said, "It is because God has made me fruitful in the land of my suffering." (Genesis 41:50–52)

In naming his sons as he did, Joseph revealed that in spite of all those nights of crying and weeping in loneliness, all those days in the dungeon, all those deep feelings of rejection and abuse, God in His grace had caused him to forget. A work of God removed the pain of the past.

Joseph refused to allow his past to be the prism through which he would view his life. His past would not be allowed to color and destroy any hope of being fruitful in his present or in his future. God caused him to forget and His grace was sufficient.

Do you live with more memories than you do dreams? Is it possible that because of what happened to you everything is colored and blurred, without focus? Does that root of bitterness spring up, and you refuse to forget and you refuse to trust God for your future?

I know a woman I'll call Maria who is in her third marriage. She's a Christian, but she has never allowed God to free her from the pain of her first marriage. The piercing rejection she suffered at the hand of an unloving husband continues to color and poison all her current relationships. She trusts no one fully. Maria has become passive-aggressive—always accusing, always second-guessing. Her present husband suffers the most from her relentless spirit of negativity. Like countless people and many Christians, Maria lives bound and embittered by the pain of her past.

Joseph escaped such bondage. He let God help him to forget. Joseph chose to live in the future and not in the past.

Recall the meaning of Joseph's second son, Ephraim: "God has made me fruitful in the land of my suffering." Perhaps you've never considered this before, but God is able to make us fruitful in the land of our suffering—the very point at which the pain is the deepest and our future most hopeless. God would never have allowed our pain if He did not intend that it bear fruit.

Many people reading this chapter have to give up their expectations that things will get better, or that their past will somehow be made right. They have to give up their dreams that their father will love them, or that a friend who has wounded them will ask forgiveness. We can't get where we need to be unless we are willing to walk away from the power of past memories and look toward the fruitfulness God can achieve in us in the days ahead—even in the land of our suffering.

2. Choose to Set Free Those Who Have Injured You

Genesis 45 tells the story. During a widespread, catastrophic famine, Joseph's brothers came to Egypt to purchase corn. They stood before Joseph but did not recognize him. Joseph tested them, to see if they were trustworthy, by keeping Simeon bound and sending the brothers back to his father and insisting that when they come the next time it had to be with their youngest brother, Benjamin. When they did finally return with Benjamin, Joseph knew it was time for him to reveal himself to them. Read this moving narrative.

> Then Joseph could no longer control himself before all his attendants, and he cried out, "Have everyone leave my presence!" So there was no one with Joseph when he made himself known to his brothers. And he wept so loudly that the Egyptians heard him, and Pharaoh's household heard about it. (Genesis 45:1–2)

Joseph wept loudly and intensely. The years of pain and bitterness he had stuffed deep into his male soul came gushing out in a flood of tears. Such tears, whether of regret over what might have been or joy over newfound forgiveness, are often necessary in the healing process. Often in the privacy of my study, I'll be talking and counseling with someone who for years has shoved the hurt and anguish and shame of past abuse by a father or sibling or someone of influence in his life deep into his soul. And almost without warning there comes a breakthrough. At once, a gush and flood of emotion erupts and he will sit for an hour or more at times and release the tears, sobbing and crying uncontrollably.

That's precisely what happened to Joseph. The emotion came out like a torrent and it prepared him for the moment of truth with his brothers.

> Then Joseph said to his brothers, "Come close to me." When they had done so, he said, "I am your brother Joseph, the one you sold into Egypt! And now, do not be distressed and do not be angry with yourselves for selling me here, because it was to save lives that God sent me ahead of you . . . God sent me ahead of you to preserve for you a remnant on earth and to save your lives by a great deliverance." (verses 4–5, 7)

Imagine, without a word of apology from his brothers, Joseph says, "Do not be distressed for what you have done . . . do not be angry with yourselves." Joseph is saying, in effect, "This is all part of God's plan for me and for you." Wow!

That's the power of releasing those who have injured you. Total exoneration—through your words to them.

If I'd been Joseph I might have been tempted to say, "I'm willing to forgive you, but let me tell you what I've been through because of you. Do you know what it was like living in a foreign

THE RIGHT RESPONSES TO INJUSTICE

Joseph shows us the correct way to respond to wrongful treatment. In his reactions to the brothers who despised and manhandled him, he chose five godly responses. We too should:

1. *Choose to live in the present and not the past.* Rather than let past injustices destroy any hope of being fruitful in the now, Joseph forgot the past and focused on the present. Through the grace of God, so can we.

2. *Choose to free those who have injured you.* Through God's grace, we can forgive even without discussing the past.

3. *Remember that in the injustice, God is present.* When God permits evil, He will use it for some higher end. We can move beyond our past when we can embrace it as part of His good plan.

4. *Choose to bless those who have wronged you.* Joseph did and Jesus commands us to (Matthew 5:44). Blessing those who have wronged you has the power to set you free.

5. *Choose not to retaliate.* Vengeance is God's business, not ours. Trust God to right all wrongs in the day of judgment.

land, being thrown unjustly into prison and tortured? Do you know . . . ?" You and I could probably have gone on for quite a while.

Joseph doesn't do that. The past is past and the future begins now. He tells his brothers not to berate themselves over the past. He is willing to forgive without even discussing the past. No need for self-incrimination.

3. Remember That in the Injustice, God Is There

In his injustice, Joseph saw God. "You sold me here but God sent me," Joseph was saying. Notice it is not just that Joseph believed that God took evil and worked it for good, but rather that *the evil of his brothers was actually a part of God's plan.* God was sovereign even over Joseph's injustice and suffering. Joseph lived many centuries before Romans 8:28 was written, and yet he understood with incredible clarity that "in all things God works for the good of those who love him." Joseph was able to see God in the midst of evil.

If all that you can see is the Devil in your injustice or abuse, you will never be free from the power of your past. You must see God too—you must see Him as permitting the evil and intending to use the evil for some higher end. We can only move beyond our past when we can embrace it as part of a plan. And while others meant it for evil, we must see it as God intending it for our good. That gives us an entirely different perspective and enables us to give praise to God—not for the evil as such but for how God will use it in our lives.

So I must ask again: Do you see God in your circumstance? Do you also see God and His providence in the evil that was done to you? God superintends our lives in order to accomplish His will. Unfortunately, we all have such enormous potential to short-circuit what God wants to do if we are determined to hang on to our bitterness. God does not leave us when we have been dealt injustice but draws near helping us accept it and move on.

Pause now and bring God into your situation by faith by giving thanks for all He is doing in your life. Thanksgiving for God's faithfulness in our pain is the indisputable proof that we believe God is a part of our pain.

4. Respond to Injustice with a Blessing

Joseph chose to offer a blessing rather than a curse. He not only had forgiven his brothers, but he offered them the invitation to return with their father, and all their children, and to live with him. In effect, he offered them the blessing of all the prosperity and comfort he enjoyed at God's favor. He could have sent them home—forgiven—but cursed to survive on their own in the middle of a severe famine. He did not. He chose to bless them rather than curse them.

You will never get at the root of your bitterness until you can bless those who have wronged you. It has the power to set you free.

I have a friend who works with Muslims in Europe seeking to bring to them the gospel of Christ. One angry Muslim wrote to him in a letter, "Cursed be you, cursed be your wife, and cursed be your children. Cursed is the home in which you live, cursed is the car that you drive." Without hesitation, my friend wrote back and offered these words: "This is my prayer for you:

blessed be your wife, blessed be your children, blessed be your home, and blessed is the car that you drive." He blessed him, just as Jesus said we should.

5. Refuse to Retaliate

Joseph refused to retaliate. Over thirty years transpired between the time Joseph was first sold into slavery and when he was reconciled to his family. That's a lot of years of living with a wrong suffered. At the end of his father's life, once again Joseph offered forgiveness and grace.

> When Joseph's brothers saw that their father was dead, they said, "What if Joseph holds a grudge against us and pays us back for all the wrongs we did to him?" So they sent word to Joseph, saying, "Your father left these instructions before he died: 'This is what you are to say to Joseph: I ask you to forgive your brothers the sins and the wrongs they committed in treating you so badly.' Now please forgive the sins of the servants of the God of your father." . . .
> But Joseph said to them, "Don't be afraid. Am I in the place of God? You intended to harm me, but God intended it for good to accomplish what is now being done, the saving of many lives." (Genesis 50:15–20)

Would Joseph retaliate? No, for that would be taking the place of God! Vengeance is God's business, not ours. It is God's work to mete out justice or mercy to those who have done wrong. You are not God, and neither am I. You cannot play God with the people who have wronged you. You are not in His place. We must trust God to bring the truth out in the open in the day of judgment and set all records straight.

Dear friend, there are situations that you simply don't need to sort out. You might want to, but you don't need to. You don't need to retaliate because you are not in the place of God. The work of bringing justice—of making right the wrong —is God's work. Your work is to forgive and release. It's the only path to healing.

Lay it all down. You do that by spending time in the presence of God and asking Him to dig out every root, every thought, every fear, every lingering shred of resentment and pain. That's God's specialty. He will "cause you to forget," and the chains will fall off. They'll fall onto the floor and you'll say, like Joseph, "I'm free—free to be blessed, free to be fruitful."

Forgiveness is both an act and a process. We choose to forgive, and when the bitterness returns we forgive again. At all costs, we must forgive or we are the losers. "Bitterness," someone has said, "is like swallowing poison and expecting your enemy to die." If you are bitter, you will die a slow death which will make your enemy happy! Forgiveness is an act of self-healing; when we forgive, we do *ourselves* a favor.

I've not come as far in my forgiveness as this prayer found in the pocket of a dead child at Ravensbruck concentration camp.

But let us pray it for ourselves:

O Lord, remember not only the men and women of good will, but also those of ill will. But do not remember all of the suffering they have inflicted upon us: Instead remember the fruits we have borne because of this suffering, our fellowship, our loyalty to one another, our humility, our courage, our generosity, the greatness of heart that has grown from this trouble. When our persecutors come to be judged by You, let all of these fruits that we have borne be their forgiveness. Amen.[1]

THE HIGH COST OF RECONCILIATION

I RECEIVED A LETTER from an African-American woman I'll call Trisha, who works in a predominantly white Christian ministry. Trisha had always thought that being a sister in Christ was stronger than race and ethnicity. But when racial comments were made by white Christians at work and she confronted the situation properly, the response was insensitive and defensive and she felt betrayed.

"To honestly talk about race and how it affects our Christianity is like taboo and unwanted, which is scary and frustrating," Trisha explained, "because it is a heart issue. I am afraid to even ask for more discussion about race with my coworkers because I fear I will find out other negative feelings about race and about me."

Let's admit that most of us who are white think that racial reconciliation has happened, but for many of our African-American brothers and sisters, racism is still alive and well. Trisha ended the letter by saying, "Unfortunately, I believe the body of Christ cannot lead the way for racial reconciliation because it is a heart issue and we live in denial on the way to heaven in spite of our heart—and this is a heart issue."

Yes, it is a heart issue, and if we don't make every effort to be reconciled we are limiting God's power and grace.

WHY RECONCILE?

For Trisha and thousands of others who want reconciliation —whether between races, family members, or fellow Christians —the question often raised is: Why bother? Why bother to reconcile? After all, there can be misunderstanding and down-right rejection when you try to restore a relationship. Here are four reasons why Christians should attempt to restore broken relationships among believers.

First, *reconciliation must be attempted because of our witness to the world.* The mark of the Christian according to Francis Schaeffer is *love*—love for one another. That's how we're known to the world—or should be. When we can't get along as Christians, it invalidates our faith. The unbelievers in the world look carefully at how Christians live and pay even closer attention to how we treat our own. Our light is supposed to shine in such a manner that people will see our attitudes in action and as a result glorify God (Matthew 5).

When unbelievers witness our divisions, our pettiness, and our anger instead, they say, "There's another good reason why

I don't need their Jesus." Whether such divisive actions or attitudes involve church members choosing sides for or against an issue or person, or involve two church members harping about each other to those in the church, trying to make listeners choose sides, the results are the same. The words and behaviors say to those on the outside: "We're not much different than any other group."

Second, *Christians pursue reconciliation in order to influence future generations.* Sadly, Christian families can be consumed and divided by conflict as well as non-Christian families. The ongoing feud between the Hatfields and the McCoys represents a humorous but sadly painful metaphor for the way many Christian families operate today. What a terrible thing to be in a family where there remains a pattern of avoiding reconciliation. Remember, what we don't forgive, we pass on. As parents, we should model love and forgiveness before our children, passing on those qualities to the next generation.

Third, *without reconciliation, there is disunity, which weakens the body of Jesus Christ.* This is why racial reconciliation is so crucial for our Christian life and witness. If we are divided over race, we prove to the world that our bond in Christ is not very strong, at least not as strong as the color of our skin or ethnic background. Racism, whether overt or skillfully hidden, is a discredit to Jesus and a blot on the body of Christ.

So is the disunity that leads to a church split. Perhaps you have witnessed the marring impact of dissension in painful church splits. When people surmise that a church split was probably of the Lord because now there are two churches, they are speaking nonsense! There are better ways to begin a church than to take advantage of an angry split. Jesus said, "If a kingdom is divided against itself, [it] cannot stand" (Mark 3:24).

Nor can a family stand that's divided against itself; father against mother, child against parent (see Mark 3:25). I'll tell you that such division—whether in the church or the home—is extremely costly. It rips, it tears, it hurts, and it weakens the body of Christ every time.

Surprisingly, many Christians believe that broken relationships are simply part of the human experience and never see the need to pursue restoration or forgiveness. That kind of indifference is contrary to the spirit of Christ. And it leaves the church weakened and, at times, ineffective in the world.

Finally, *reconciled Christians demonstrate the power of Christ's gospel.* Reconciliation represents the very core of the Christian message. When we pray for a person because he has cancer and he is healed, a secular doctor does not accept our interpretation. He's seen many remarkable recoveries without any reference to God and prayer. But when a bitter couple reconciles, when a church has a reconciliation service after a split, then it is more difficult to deny that this is of God. Read how the apostle Paul describes the powerful notion of Christian reconciliation.

> Therefore, if anyone is in Christ, he is a new creation; the old has gone, the new has come! All this is from God, who reconciled us to himself through Christ and gave us the ministry of reconciliation: that God was reconciling the world to himself in Christ, not counting men's sins against them. And he has committed to us the message of reconciliation. (2 Corinthians 5:17–19)

THE POWER THAT TRANSFORMS

This is the power that transforms. Genuine reconciliation brings transformation because it comes from God. America will never have a great revival unless we have estranged couples reconciled, falling in love again. In spite of unfaithfulness and everything you can imagine, they must stand and testify, "We were on the brink of divorce. But Christ broke into our marriage and here we stand today loving each other, fully reconciled."

That is the power of the Gospel! Every revival that I've ever studied always has believers' reconciliation as paramount.

In the early 1970s in Canada, a spiritual revival began when two brothers who had not spoken to each other for twenty years were reconciled. Their pastor had taken them to the church basement, surrounded them with praying deacons, and then insisted that they stay until they were willing to lay down their bitterness. After a time there was deep repentance and restoration, and the next evening the brothers sang a duet in the church. This ignited a spiritual awakening that spread to hundreds of churches. There were hundreds of stories of reconciliation—parents with teenagers, husbands and wives and relatives and church members.[1] Reconciliation is always a by-product of the work of the Holy Spirit. It gives compelling evidence to the power of the Gospel. When the Spirit moves, reconciliation can be found.

Clearly, true reconciliation is born of the Holy Spirit. Yet to accomplish genuine reconciliation, there are still steps to follow, which are outlined by our Lord. Taken together, with a true reliance on God's gracious power, reconciliation can come about and relationships can be restored.

SIX STEPS TO GENUINE RECONCILIATION

In Matthew 18 and Galatians 6 we find six steps for genuine reconciliation. They are intensely practical and they are sequential. Both are important to understand as we look more closely at each step. These are the words of Jesus on the matter of reconciliation:

> If your brother sins against you, go and show him his fault, just between the two of you. If he listens to you, you have won your brother over. But if he will not listen, take one or two others along, so that every matter may be established by the testimony of two or three witnesses. If he refuses to listen to them, tell it to the church; and if he refuses to listen even to the church, treat him as you would a pagan or a tax collector. (Matthew 18:15–17)

1. Prepare Your Heart

Before you go to the other person, get ready. The first step in seeking reconciliation is to prayerfully prepare your heart. Look at the apostle Paul's wise counsel in Galatians 6:1: "Brothers, if someone is caught in a sin, you who are spiritual should restore him gently. But watch yourself, or you also may be tempted."

Paul understood the nature of the human heart. It's impulsive, deceitful, and given to self-serving motives. That's why he established that the process of reconciliation is a profoundly spiritual exercise. You must "pray up," as one of my pastor friends would say, before you do anything. The point is to make certain your heart is in tune with the Spirit before you make a move toward the erring party. Left to yourself you will likely overcorrect or intensify the conflict because you'll be relying on your own emotions or perspective. Notice for Paul the guiding principle is gentleness, which of course, is a fruit of the Spirit (Galatians 5:23). To "restore" is a verb that describes the setting of a broken bone. You are going to the other person in tenderness and with a gentle spirit.

Preparing your heart also assures that you see the matter purely as God sees it. It is so easy to be blind to your own faults and even your role in the breakdown. Especially if you have been sinned against, you need to guard against selfishness or vengeance. You must go with the full knowledge that *you are capable of doing exactly what the offender has done!*

2. Make the Initial Contact in Private

Second, you go privately and confront the one who has wronged you. And you go with the intention of reconciling, not exposing what happened. Jesus said, "If your brother sins against you go and show him his fault." Too many people make the mistake of waiting for the guilty party to make the first move. Rarely will that happen. Jesus urged the one who had been sinned against to gently and humbly approach the other. By the way, that means resisting the temptation to talk about your situation or the wrong done to you with others. That's gossip, plain and simple. And the Bible has one word for that: *sin.* Don't go there! Don't go to the telephone, don't gossip, don't slander, and don't say things about people that are negative, even if they are true, unless the person to whom you are speaking is either part of the problem or part of the solution.

Twenty-five years ago a young Bible college student came to accuse a religious leader of subtle dishonesty. Whether the story was true or not made no difference, but often when I meet that evangelical leader I still think of the slanderous implications of what my friend said. My advice: Be careful with your tongue, for it is set on the fire of hell. (See the warning of the apostle James in James 3:2–12, especially verse 6.)

Pastor Jim Cymbala of the Brooklyn Tabernacle in New York believes that the sin of gossip was virtually eliminated from their congregation as each new member made a promise not to spread bad reports about anyone in the church, but to go to that person and clear up the matter. That's a powerful commitment. Don't lash out publicly at the person who hurt you. Jesus said, "Go in private, alone, and with gentleness and humility." That's great counsel.

There may be one exception to going alone—when the person you need to confront is a dangerous, unpredictable character. You would be wise perhaps to take along someone for safety purposes and accountability. That exception may particularly apply when a minor is involved and needs to confront an adult or peer. But if it is possible, in most instances, go alone and resolve the issue privately.

One of the most difficult counseling situations in my ministry was when I was present as a wife had to tell her husband that their second child wasn't his. You can imagine the shock, the betrayal, and the unanswered questions that revelation brought to the surface. The woman could not take the lies and deceit any longer; the truth had to come out despite the consequences. She wanted and needed his forgiveness, and she wanted me to be present, fearing his response.

I listened and then tried to persuade the husband to embrace a large dose of the grace of God and accept this child as his own. He agreed to do that initially. Years later I heard they divorced.

My point is simply there are times when we need others present in the counseling setting. When there is a confrontation that could have damaging consequences, it would be wise to take someone else with you.

3. Evaluate Each Response

As you proceed through the process, take time prayerfully to evaluate the response of the one you confront. At times the person you are seeking to restore may not even realize he or she hurt you. Probably nine out of ten times if you go to a person and say, "You know, you've hurt me deeply," they will be surprised. Human nature reveals that at the end of the day we're all somewhat narcissistic. We don't even realize how we hurt other people by what we say or what we do. We fail to see them as they see themselves.

Remember, Jesus says, "If he listens to you, you have won your brother over."

If reconciliation is made, that ends the matter. Nobody else needs to know. If it's not, then another step is required.

THE RIGHT ATTITUDES

The steps that Jesus outlines for reconciliation help us develop the right attitudes in approaching the one who offended us. Through these steps we are able to come to the other person with an attitude of

- *gentleness,* like one who is tenderly seeking to heal a broken bone.
- *humility,* aware that we are capable of doing exactly what the offender has done and that we may have even contributed to the offense.
- *introspection,* searching our own heart for self–serving motives and recognizing that the human heart is impulsive and deceitful. (Remember that the process of reconciliation is a profoundly spiritual exercise, requiring prayer.)
- *love,* seeking the best for the relationship and avoiding gossip that would damage the other person (even if the potentially damaging statements are true).

4. Enlist the Help of Others

If after going privately to the offending individual you receive no recognizable response, you must consider bringing others into the loop. That's what Jesus meant when He said, "But if he will not listen, take one or two others along, so that 'every matter may be established by the testimony of two or three witnesses'" (Matthew 18:16). By bringing witnesses you are able to clarify the issues. It's possible an outside perspective might alone diffuse the situation and reveal your flawed perspective. But also, bringing others with you helps confirm the issues at the heart of the conflict. Someone else will hear things differently than you because they are more emotionally objective. Because the potential fifth step is much more severe and public, providing two or three witnesses to the seriousness of the situation protects you from becoming more vulnerable.

I know a man who sponsored an annual Bible conference at the school where he served as president. One year he advertised a certain preacher who would be the featured speaker. Somebody called the school and made some startling accusations about the preacher—calling him an adulterer. The wise administrator listened but did not respond. The guest speaker came and spoke as scheduled and enjoyed a fruitful ministry. In the days following the conference the individual who first made the charges called back and confessed he had had the wrong person. What a terrible debacle was avoided on the principle of requiring a second (or even a third) witness.

Pay close attention to this next sentence: *It would be better for you to play with forked lightning than to slander a believer and make false charges against a brother or sister in Christ.* Having two or three witnesses to collaborate your report keeps the matter above reproach.

I need to pause and make a very candid observation. There are many people who do not want to become members of a local body of believers because they prefer to be like a bottle without a label, easily drifting from place to place without ever dropping anchor. We, like other churches, have many attenders at Moody

Church who don't want to become members because they know this implies accountability. Yet, that accountability is a blanket of security. Without it we can more easily go astray.

5. Bring the Matter to the Church

Where reconciliation does not take place even with others present, Jesus said that the next step is to "tell it to the church," and have them go and convince him otherwise.

This is perhaps the most difficult and painful step in the process of reconciliation. I hope you will never have to resort to such a dramatic and agonizing ordeal. But the provision is made for the stubborn soul who refuses to repent and be reconciled.

I remember on one occasion at Moody Church we had about fifteen members of our executive committee go to a fellow believer on the executive team who was involved in an adulterous relationship. We pled with the man to break off the relationship and come back to the Lord. He refused our pleadings. Bringing the church into the process gives the body a chance to heal itself, or if not, to participate at least indirectly in taking out a cancer that could hurt the whole body. Painful yes, but we never regretted the decision. It was the next step in the process as outlined by the Lord.

Now if the sinning brother doesn't repent at this point, it is usually because his heart has grown hard. That's especially true in matters of immorality. A man or woman feels he or she has invested too much in the adulterous relationship that they cannot bring themselves to simply walk away and be done with it. The marriage bed is defiled and that's an extremely difficult injury from which to recover.

I recall one Christian leader saying to me as I was pleading with him to go back to his wife, "You know, even David got his Bathsheba!" Such blindness! Sure David got Bathsheba, but along with her came a world and lifetime of heartache. David died a broken man, whose household had been torn apart because of his sin four of his sons died in subsequent conflicts and his own kingdom overturned by Absalom his son. And—his heart was ruptured by the death of his infant son by Bathsheba. A heavy price to pay for a few moments of sexual pleasure!

Even when the matter goes public to the church, the individual may be so hardened by his rebellion that a more dramatic step must be taken.

6. Excommunication from the Fellowship

If after the above steps there is still no repentance, the sinning individual must be removed from the fellowship. He or she is to be considered and treated as a pagan—one who willingly refuses to acknowledge God. By putting someone out of the fellowship, you are removing them from the gracious umbrella of God's protection—they become alarmingly vulnerable to Satan's assaults. The goal remains reconciliation, but the means grow more dramatic and intense with each ensuing step.

Keep in mind two truths in moving to this final step: (1) We do not excommunicate repentant sinners but only unrepentant ones; and (2) the sin may not involve a church leader; it may be a husband or wife or single person. Importantly, the person has gone through the prior steps without repentance and has an attitude of rebellion. Whoever comes to this final step does so because his or her sin is affecting the church. This final step shows the church body that the church honors God's commands and that unrepentant sin against the church must be resolved by removal from the church.

Sometimes the discipline of excommunication has the desired effect, but at times it is not effective and the disciplined person dies in rebellion. In other instances it takes days or weeks, even years, but eventually individuals removed from fellowship realize the error of their ways. Ten years after we removed one man from the church membership, he wrote me a long letter, in which he detailed all that he'd been through since he turned his back on our pleadings. He told about how severely God disciplined him for his disobedience and how his hard heart had to be broken into submission.

Hopefully, the pain and remorse of public rejection and humiliation brings a man or woman into submission, but if not, God will do it in His own way. All the while, the path back is kept groomed and lighted 24/7, just in case the brother or sister decides to repent and come home—which leads us to the final step.

CONTINUE IN PRAYER FOR RECONCILIATION

We must never give up hope that one day reconciliation will be accomplished. Prayer keeps hope alive. No matter how bleak the situation or how long the wait, prevailing prayer is our best hope in bringing about genuine reconciliation. If the brother is restored, tell the church. Celebrate. Rejoice, even throw a party! Ultimately, the work of restoration belongs to God and Him alone.

When reconciliation doesn't happen, you must still forgive those who have wronged you. They may go to their grave refusing to acknowledge what they've done, but that does not exempt you from forgiving the wrong. Let's face it; when trust is eroded reconciliation is nearly impossible. And when it can't be accomplished, you can still forgive.

THE COST OF RECONCILIATION

When you grant someone forgiveness, you set the person free, but that forgiveness might cost you plenty. When Jesus told the parable of the man who owed the king ten thousand talents, the king graciously forgave him. Forgiveness was free to the servant, but at the end of the fiscal year, the king had to absorb the huge cost. A wife may forgive her husband for adultery; the forgiveness is free to him, but it costs her distress, humiliation, and the deep feelings of betrayal.

In his book *Let Justice Roll Down,* John Perkins writes compellingly about the work God did in his heart to bring about a spirit of forgiveness toward those who had wronged him so deeply.

The Spirit of God worked on me as I lay in that bed. An image formed in my mind, the image of the cross, Christ on the cross. I blotted out everything else in my mind. . . . Jesus knew what I suffered. He understood, He cared, and He'd experienced it all.

This Jesus, this one who had brought good news directly from God in heaven had lived what He preached. Yet He was arrested, falsely accused. Like me,

He went through an unjust trial; He also faced a lynch mob and got beaten. But even more than that, He was nailed to rough wooden planks and killed. Killed like a common criminal.

At the crucial moment, it seemed that even God Himself had deserted Him. . . .

But when He looked at that mob who had lynched Him, He didn't hate them. He loved them. He forgave them. And He prayed to God to forgive them. "Father, forgive these people, for they don't know what they are doing."

His enemies hated. But Jesus forgave. I couldn't get away from that.

The Spirit of God kept working on me and in me until I could say with Jesus, "I forgive them, too." I promised Him that I would "return good for evil," not evil for evil. And He gave me the love I knew I would need to fulfill His command to me of "love your enemy."

Because of Christ, God Himself met me and healed my heart and my mind with His love. I knew then what Paul meant when he wrote, "Who shall separate us from the love of Christ?"[2]

God has used John Perkins mightily to bring reconciliation within the body of Christ. His powerful forgiveness has enabled him to walk through many doors that otherwise would be closed. Forgiveness is the trigger that releases God's power and demonstrates the truth of the gospel.

We can also learn a lesson from evangelist Sammy Tippet. He attended high school in Baton Rouge, Louisiana, when racial tension was at its height. When four African-American girls had the courage to attend the all-white school, they endured humiliation, racial slurs, and bitter innuendo. On one occasion, Tippet recalls more than a hundred students screaming and yelling as they surrounded one of these girls during the lunch hour while she held her head in her hands and wept. Sammy knew that no human being should be treated like that, so he did not participate, but he was a coward and did nothing.

Years later, he was converted to Christ and God radically changed his heart, delivering him from the curse of racism. Sometime after this, God burdened his heart to pray that God would give him the opportunity of asking these girls for forgiveness for his cowardice and to apologize for what they endured at the school. But how to find them? He had no way to make contact. He surmised that by now they were married and living who knows where. But year after year he prayed that God would connect him with them.

When his daughter-in-law, Kelly, got information on the Internet to set up a CPR training class for the family now living in San Antonio, the teacher was African-American. She began, "If you don't understand my accent it's because I grew up in Baton Rouge."

Sammy's heart skipped at the words. He figured that she was about his age. Could this be an answer to his twenty-one-year prayer? He spoke to her after the training—yes, she was one of those girls! He fumbled for words, apologizing for the way she was treated and then followed up with a detailed e-mail, begging her forgiveness.

She replied, "I always remember those days, not with bitterness but with sadness. On behalf of my colleagues I accept your apology, and most importantly, God accepts your apology. Thank you for being a true leader and speaking up now. The sadness I felt turned to joy knowing that there are people like you, lovers of God, making this right and making the world make sense."[3]

God will rearrange schedules and overcome barriers in ways that we did not think possible when we are serious about reconciliation. Reconciliation helps all of us make sense of the world. God answers prayers for reconciliation because He is in the reconciliation business.

Remember these words of Jesus were given in the context of reconciliation: "Where two or three are gathered together in My name, I am there in the midst of them" (Matthew 18:20 NKJV).

WHEN RECONCILIATION ~~FAILS~~

I'D LIKE YOU TO READ THIS HAUNTING E-MAIL I received from a prison volunteer not long ago:

"Walking down a metal catwalk past prison cells of convicts is an incredible experience. It was in the spirit of adventure that I was followed by a blue uniformed guard as we approached the stairwell. Then we met the serpentine corridors and vacated courtyards. Each lower floor level became darker, dirtier, and more austere until we leveled off on a dingy walkway, with the strongest aroma of stench I have ever smelled. This was the dungeon within the dungeon, for detention, for the most evil offenders.

"The cells were drab with bricked in windows; no cot, sink, or toilet. A hole in the floor dropped directly into the cesspool that was rumored to back up regularly into these cells. This was the home of those who were ill-suited to live with other residents.

"The officer was determined to hustle me out of this 'no visitor' area. The men were strangely hushed, either seated on the floor or standing up with a drugged, glazed look in their eyes. No radio, no television, or even idle chatter. A thick cloud of oppression; Satan was there.

"One of these pathetic captives caught my attention," the prison volunteer continued in his e-mail narrative. "He was crouched like a creature on the cement floor. He wore only his grossly stained underwear and his hair was standing out in a frightful, wild fashion. His eyes were bulging and hollow, his fingers were long, and his matted beard barely hid his rotted teeth and infected mouth.

"I spoke, 'You need to accept Christ as your Savior and Lord.' He didn't rouse. I cried out again, 'Jesus is your only salvation. It's time to repent and receive Jesus.' He turned and looked me full in the face, but gave no inclination of reply.

"Finally, the guard angrily took my arm to keep me moving, so I shouted behind me, 'Why won't you do this?' And he shouted back, 'I'm not ready to give it all up yet.' And with that he was out of sight."

How stubborn at times is the human heart! I thought, reading that e-mail.

Even after reading seven fairly intense chapters on the need and process of reconciliation, it's possible that you, like that tormented prisoner, aren't yet ready to give it all up. Perhaps you are hanging on to offenses and to a painful past. William Henley wrote,

Out of the night that covers me,
Black as the pit from pole to pole,
I thank whatever gods there be
For my unconquerable soul.

Those are the defiant opening lines from *Invictus*, written in 1875. They are also the last will and testament of convicted Oklahoma City bomber Timothy McVeigh (described in the opening paragraphs of chapter 3). Even facing execution, McVeigh remained unmoved. His stubborn heart refused to give in.

I recall a man telling me that he wanted to wait to receive Christ as Savior until after his parents were both dead, so as not to give them the satisfaction of knowing he became a Christian! He harbored such an ugly, relentless grudge. At the heart of such stubbornness are a series of lies bought into by the human soul—lies about who God is and about our being entitled to personal justice. Those lies keep people in bondage to their pain and their shame. People who are hurting are very susceptible to believing lies.

Before we identify the lies and how to overcome them, let's look at the goal: reconciliation. Of course, full reconciliation is the goal, but sometimes we cannot achieve total reconciliation.

KINDS OF RECONCILIATION

Full Reconciliation

Full reconciliation can occur when trust, honesty, and respect are all present; it happens when forgiveness restores the implicit belief that two people, or classes of people, have been brought together in faith, each concerned about the welfare of the other. When trust, forgiveness, or respect is lacking, it is difficult to move ahead in a meaningful relationship.

Full reconciliation is possible even under difficult circumstances. A barrier that destroys one marriage can at times strengthen another. I know a man who confessed his infidelity to his wife. As he approached her, he feared that this admission would break up their marriage. Nevertheless, he did what was necessary. His admission had the opposite effect—it opened their marriage to a whole new level of communication and honesty. After twenty years on emotional autopilot, they finally became genuine about their feelings and fears. Each was willing to share their inmost struggles, the disappointments, and the pain.

Obviously, the sin of adultery is not the answer to marital discord; almost always it breaks up a marriage. But sometimes people need a wake-up call to make those changes they should have made long ago. This is proof that almost any barrier can be overcome if the parties have humility, trust, and respect. Honesty must be up-front and center.

I've seen full reconciliation in church relationships where there has been forgiveness and a deep commitment to set differences aside for the sake of mutual harmony and the good of the entire body. Conflict often is the result of territorialism, jealousy and the need to be 'right' about everything. Thus true repentance often brings about reconciliation.

And if respect and trust are lacking? These can be rebuilt over a period of time if there is the commitment and willingness to do so. Nowhere is this more true than in the marriage relationship. Given time and hard work, trust can be restored and time, wisely spent, can heal many wounds. If not, there can be partial reconciliation, which is preferable to no reconciliation at all, but it lacks a deep commitment on both sides.

Partial Reconciliation

Second, there is what I call *partial reconciliation*. This happens when there is a recognition of wrongdoing; forgiveness has been both requested and received, but trust and respect have been so seriously eroded that there cannot be any real in-depth friendship. Consider the man who commits adultery and asks his wife for forgiveness, and because she is a Christian she grants it. He does not deeply repent, but he expects life to continue as if nothing happened . . . after all, he asked for forgiveness and received it. But it is clear he does not understand the enormity of his sin; he does not understand the depth of the pain and hurt that he caused. If we trivialize what the other party considers serious, there cannot be full reconciliation. Keep in mind that *when sin is viewed superficially, it is dealt with superficially.*

Partial reconciliation also comes about where the real fruit of repentance is lacking. Where little effort is made to rectify the wrong, or to change behavior, then the relationship will always be suspect. There are some people with whom we find it difficult to bond; so much has happened, the feelings run so deep that the best we can do is accept one another and move on, even without a close, trusting relationship.

If an uncle were to molest one of your children, you would report him to the authorities and he would have to accept the legal consequences of what he has done. In the future, if he is repentant, perhaps a cordial relationship can eventually be developed; there can be reconciliation of sorts. But would you trust him with your children again? *Never.*

Probably there are many people in our past with whom we are partially reconciled: there is a cordial relationship, a mutual commitment to treat one another with respect, but the memories of the past make us wary and cautious. And of course, sometimes there are personality differences that make it difficult to be in full fellowship with others. Let us also remember that others might think about us what we think about them! Perhaps we have eroded their trust or been unfair in our past dealings. Whenever possible, we should do what we can to make partial reconciliation full reconciliation.

No Reconciliation

We've already emphasized that you cannot reconcile with a spear thrower or a destroyer. David could never have reconciled with Saul. "My mother in law is a spear thrower" a letter sent to me began. "She tries to control us, our children and even our schedules. My husband realizes this, and we've had to just back off and draw some boundaries." Perhaps it is possible in a such a situation to have partial reconciliation, but we cannot reconcile with those who seek our undoing.

There cannot be reconciliation with a person who believes that your forgiveness wipes out his or her legitimate debts. I'm talking about the attitude of the person who says, "If you forgive me, I should not have to repay the money I owe." Or, the person who says, "If you forgive me, I should not have to go to jail."

In one highly publicized court case, the plaintiff was all

too eager to accept the forgiveness of a Christian couple, thinking that this should end the criminal proceedings against him. "They forgave me" he said, thinking that this gave him a "get out of jail free" card. But forgiveness does not wipe out the natural and necessary consequences of wrongdoing. Even when God forgives us, we still have to endure the results of what we've done. Just ask David, whose repentance reconciled him to God, but nonetheless his sin destroyed him and his family.

Also, you can't reconcile with a person who has died, or a person who would only use your request for forgiveness as another reason to prove that you are totally wrong and he is totally innocent. Confront some people with what they have done and they will resort to total denial; they are so incapable of seeing their sin that further discussion is a waste of time. Let me say it again, that when understanding and trust are seriously eroded there is little hope that reconciliation can take place.

If you must live in close proximity to those with whom reconciliation has failed, you have inner, God-given resources to cope victoriously in such circumstances. For one thing, don't let the controlling person—the person who refuses rational reconciliation—don't let him/her define you. You are responsible for yourself, not the difficult people who happen to be in your life, either by necessity or by choice. Don't give this person ownership of your feelings. You must be in control of who you are and what God has called you to do.

Second, almost always there is no use trying to change the opinions of the person who won't reconcile. Most such people are very content with their viewpoint; more accurately, they are convinced that theirs is the only opinion that matters. Since they have no interest in the truth but only in proclaiming their version of it, you must entrust them solely to God. As for you, stop watering silk flowers.

Seek God for wisdom. Just as God was there for David when Saul was chasing him, just so God is there for us when we encounter difficult people who refuse all counsel, whether it comes from us or from others. Our responsibility is to be a healthy, godly, Spirit-filled person, and God uses these situations to develop qualities we'd never otherwise have.

However, when reconciliation fails, that does not mean that our duty is over. We must release the bitterness and *not let other people's sin ruin our lives.*

THE ROLE OF ONE-SIDED FORGIVENESS

Yes, I believe in what I call one-sided forgiveness. Bitterness must be released from our lives, or we are the losers. If you have been offended, you need to forgive the one who has wronged you. When we don't forgive those who have wronged us, our lives will remain under the control of those who have done us the most damage. Let me say it again: Don't let their sin ruin your life.

What to do then? What if you've been hurt by a destroyer (chapter 3) or a spear thrower (chapter 5)? In that situation you are particularly vulnerable to lies that the Devil would like to implant in your soul. He would like to hold you bound so that you stay in your prison, unable to get beyond the past to a better future. We will look at Satan's three big lies, for they tell us *what not to do* and *what not to believe.* Then we will answer that key question: What should I do when there is no reconciliation?

SATAN'S BIG LIES

Lie number one: "God doesn't care about my pain." Those who believe this lie tell themselves, *If God cared He would have judged the person who has wounded me; instead, He has postponed His justice for some elusive future date. I won't wait for that.*

"There can't be a God who cares," one woman said to me, because of the endless devastation her ex-husband had inflicted upon the family and on others. If God were in heaven and were the least bit loving, she argued, none of this injustice would have been suffered, and if it had happened, justice would not be slow in coming. This lie strikes at the heart of our belief that God is good and He cares for us.

R. T. Kendall is right when he says, "Although we often do not see it at first, all of our bitterness is ultimately traceable to a resentment of God."[1] *Thus, when we forgive others, we must also let go of our bitterness toward God.*

Lie number two: "If I'm hurting, I'm justified in making everyone around me equally miserable." How sad is this deception. The idea is that if you're hurting, everyone else must hurt too. It's the law of misery loving company—but rather, it's misery *demanding* company.

Many angry parents have overcorrected their children while angry or bitter; thus, they are passing their hurt to a future generation. The long-term effects of our bitterness can affect people whom we shall never meet.

Lie number three: "When I forgive, I minimize the wrong I've suffered." Not true. The injustice is no less when you forgive; God recognizes the injustice. But even if reconciliation is not possible, there is a kind of one-sided forgiveness that you must experience to set yourself free. And granting that forgiveness in the presence of God does not trivialize the enormity of the injustice you have experienced.

We must recognize these lies and reject each one as a falsehood hindering our ability to forgive an offense. When reconciliation fails, we must recall the one overarching truth: We must forgive the offender.

WHAT TO DO WHEN RECONCILIATION FAILS

Forgiveness is releasing the bitterness in spite of the pain. Don't deny the pain; rather, forgive in the midst of the pain. I recently heard of a young man who started his own company and soon afterward formed a board of incorporated members. His board included members of his immediate family. Eventually, motivated by greed, the family members turned against him and plotted a hostile takeover of his company. The young man struggles to this day with the prospect of forgiving and forgetting the injustice he suffered by those closest to him. But thankfully, he has chosen to forgive even when reconciliation is not possible.

When you forgive you do not minimize the hurt, the pain, or the evil. What you do is release it into the Lord's capable and loving hands. As we noted in the previous chapter, He is the perfect judge and ultimate keeper of justice.

Refusing to believe the lies means leaving it all to Him and focusing on the truth. The truth is found in the pages of

God's Word, and more specifically in one of my favorite passages of Paul's letter to the Romans.

THE TRUTH WILL SET YOU FREE

For those caught in the web of Satan's lies, what's needed is a strong dose of divine truth. For that we go to the powerful passage in Romans 12 where Paul provides the secret to leaving your past behind and moving to a future of joy and usefulness.

> Love must be sincere. Hate what is evil; cling to what is good. Be devoted to one another in brotherly love. Honor one another above yourselves. Never be lacking in zeal, but keep your spiritual fervor, serving the Lord. Be joyful in hope, patient in affliction, faithful in prayer. Share with God's people who are in need. Practice hospitality.
>
> Bless those who persecute you; bless and do not curse. Rejoice with those who rejoice; mourn with those who mourn. Live in harmony with one another. Do not be proud, but be willing to associate with people of low position. Do not be conceited.
>
> Do not repay anyone evil for evil. Be careful to do what is right in the eyes of everybody. If it is possible, as far as it depends on you, live at peace with everyone. Do not take revenge, my friends, but leave room for God's wrath, for it is written: "It is mine to avenge; I will repay," says the Lord. . . .
>
> Do not be overcome by evil, but overcome evil with good. (Romans 12:9–21)

Truth Expressed

In this passage Paul addressed the antidote for human conflict—selfless humility, forgiveness, and restraint.

Here we find three action steps, each representing the truth that counteracts Satan's lies.

First, *we can counteract lies by what we say.* To those caught in the press of personal conflict, Jesus said to "bless those who curse you, . . . and pray for those who spitefully use you and persecute you" (Matthew 5:44 NKJV; compare with Romans 12:14). Words are the vehicle for both blessings and curses. Jesus said you counteract lies by expressing truthful words. Bless those who persecute you.

You say, "Well, how do we do that?" First, you pray for them a prayer of blessing, not vengeance. Second, you speak well of them both in private and public. No matter how troublesome your enemy there is something good to be said about him.

Confederate General Robert E. Lee spoke in the highest terms to President Lincoln about an officer who was known to have nothing but hatred and disrespect for him (that is, for Robert E. Lee), his commanding officer. When someone pointed out to the general the contempt this man had for him, General Lee replied, "Yes, that's true. But the President asked my opinion of him, not his opinion of me." That's blessing, not cursing, and it's a powerful antidote for bitterness.

I was surprised to hear a woman who was sexually abused by her father say, "There are many ways in which my father was a good man." Then she began to list his hard work, care for the family, and helpfulness in time of need. I was impressed that this woman did not allow the evil that her father did to blot out any good he might have accomplished. I believe God rewards those who find something good to say, even about those who have wronged us.

Second, *we can express truth by how we feel*—by exhibiting appropriate emotions. Jesus said, "Rejoice with those who rejoice; mourn with those who mourn." Is it harder to rejoice with those who rejoice or to weep with those who weep? Certainly you and I find it harder to rejoice with those who rejoice—especially those individuals we consider our enemies.

HOW TO COUNTER SATAN'S LIES

Here are the three action steps, each representing the truth that counteracts Satan's lies:

1. *Speak* words of blessing to those who persecute you. Though it will be difficult, you can find something good to say even about those who have wronged you.
2. *Feel* the emotions of your adversary, the person with whom, at present, you are unable to reconcile. Recognize that you also could act in such a way, and enter into their pain.
3. *Act* in a way that promotes harmony and makes restoration possible. Resist the temptation to get even, gossip, or throw criticism toward the offender. Remember the goal is to "live at peace with everyone," even those who have wronged us.

When you open the morning paper and read of the tragic death of a local teenager, your heart goes out to the grieving family. I can't imagine the horror of receiving a call in the early morning hours informing you of the death of your teenage son or daughter. We find it easy to share in the pain and sorrow of such families, no matter who they are. But let those same people be promoted above us; let them receive special recognition for their character, and that's a different story! It's hard for you to rejoice when your friends unexpectedly inherit a million dollars; it is doubly more difficult to rejoice if the person who received it was an enemy!

But I believe Jonathan Edwards was correct when he said, "In heaven when we see people exalted above us, we will rejoice as if their exaltation were our own." Most people want to weep when their enemy rejoices, and rejoice when their enemy suffers. We relish the thought of an enemy getting his just reward. Yet, that's not the way of the Spirit; that's the impulse of the flesh.

Try for a moment to enter into the world of that person with whom you cannot reconcile, your adversary. Keep in mind that you are capable of doing what he/she has done. Yes, the potential of evil—great evil—exists in us all. For a moment, enter into their sorrows, their disappointments, and their pain. For a moment, weep with the person who weeps and rejoice with the person who rejoices.

Third, *we believe the truth by what we do.* Truth is perhaps best expressed in our actions. Paul says, "Live in harmony with one another. Do not be proud, but be willing to associate with people of low position . . . do not repay anyone evil for evil" (Romans 12:16–17). The emphasis in Paul's final exhortations is on actions—the kind of actions that always reflect a self-less, harmonious existence with other believers. Conceit makes us rejoice when our enemy weeps. Humility allows us to act like Christ—selflessly rejoicing with those who rejoice.

Such humility means we resist the temptation to get even, to speak our mind or retaliate with a finely prepared excoriating rebuke. None of that brings reconciliation. The goal for the Christian, with God's help, is to "live at peace with everyone," including with those who've wronged us.

Sound impossible? At times it is. That's because there are impossible people. Still, I urge you not to avenge yourselves, but rather in humility and trust, "leave room for the wrath of God."

So much for the negative. That's Paul's list of don'ts in regard to our actions. He also offers a list of dos (in verses 20–21):

- If your enemy is hungry, feed him.
- If your enemy is thirsty, give him something to drink.
- Overcome all evil with good.

When you act like that, you actually can bring shame and possibly repentance to your enemy by "heaping coals" of guilt on his head. As a boy on our farm, I remember a particularly difficult neighbor. In the fall when the fields had been harvested, some of our cattle would wander on to the old man's property. His anger would burn and he'd curse anyone who was within earshot.

One day some of his horses got loose and came across the fence into one of my dad's fields. What I remember is how kindly we caught those animals and took them back to our grumpy neighbor without saying a word. He felt embarrassed and ashamed. Instead of retaliating, we acted kindly and in humility.

LET THE CHAINS FALL OFF

I'm told that when a rattlesnake is cornered it will sometimes bite itself. This self-inflicted punishment is perhaps done in anger or as a form of vengeance, but it hurts only the snake. Just so bitterness is a self-inflicted wound that hurts us but is of no concern to our enemy. I don't know how to say it more strongly: We must let go of the bitterness and revenge that contaminates our souls. We are needlessly hurting ourselves.

One morning while driving to the office, I listened to a broadcast on a local radio station. A woman read a penetrating piece about the debilitating power of resentment. Here are the words of Roma Wade, a talk show cohost on Chicago's WLS-AM radio.

Do you harbor resentment?

Then you are poisoning your own meal at life's banquet table. Imagine your mind as a "little shop of horrors," a kind of museum filled with relics of all the injustices and harm you've ever endured. Each exhibit depicts your memory of what someone did or didn't do that hurt you. Brightly illuminated by your resentment, every exhibit has a sound track echoing with loud, angry, and accusing voices. The walls are covered with horrible instruments of punishment and long lists of penalties to be inflicted on your wrongdoers. And coating everything is a think, clinging residue of self-pity that keeps you from moving along to the New Futures Wing of your museum—where the exhibits are filled with pleasure and joy—and possibilities.

Can you imagine what it would be like to be locked permanently inside such a chamber of horror and hate and resentment? If you are unable to forgive others for real or imagined wrongs then that horror chamber exists within YOU. That chamber of Ill Will is YOUR OWN MIND.

And what a price you pay for maintaining such a museum of resentment! The negative reliving of your past stokes anger, resentment, and seething hostility. It also turns your mind against itself. It is like poison to your soul. The simple, profound truth is that the entire horror shop crumbles if you simply FORGIVE. By forgiving others you forgive yourself and you gain self-esteem, and you free your own spirit to soar to new heights.

There is no time to waste. Now is the time to stop the pain of the past from poisoning the joys of your present and your future.

Decide to FORGIVE and then LET GO.[2]

I happened to e-mail this illustration to someone later that day. His reply included a description of his own pain and how he ended the poisoning:

There was such a chamber in my soul and the pain etched itself deep into the grooves of my mind. A godly person helped me to bridge the way to the new future's wing of my life's museum. Her soul care advised that my pain needed a voice. As long as I ignored the pain, it was like looking into a mirror and not seeing a reflection of something that was very real. So one day I had a funeral service for my dreams of childhood that died, and the loving ideas I had about my mom and dad. I had to die to those. The reality was that my mom and dad left bleeding lashes on the face of my soul. That day I took flowers to the chosen grave site, and a candle. I placed the flowers on the ground and blew out the candle of hope; the hope that my parents would rise to meet me at the level of my dreams.

I invited God to the ceremony that day and shed my tears in His presence. I knew the pain would echo into the future in days to come, so I asked God to just help me suffer well, and trust Him for how He would redeem my future. It has been a long obedience in the same direction over many years, and God has been faithful indeed. The pain is still there on occasion. But the pain and the anger have lost their power over me. The wound has become a scar *because healing has taken place.* (emphasis added)

Dear friend, if you are right now holding tighter to your bitterness from a wrong you've suffered than you are to this book, I urge you to lay down the book and surrender your pain to Christ. Only He is able to set you free from the prison of resentment. Don't allow the foolish, petty deeds of a long lost enemy chain you to a life of misery and anger. Your marriage has suffered long enough; your children have endured the brunt of your angry outbursts for too long already; your ministry is dangling by a very thin thread. Give it up now. Let your wounds become scars and start living again. Will you do that today? I pray that you will.

Recall again the warning: "Bitterness is like drinking poison and expecting your enemy to die!" Of course, the poison hurts you, not the one whom you hate.

Are you ready to "give it all up"?

NOTES

Chapter 2: The Blinding Power of an Offense

1. Steve Gallagher, *At the Altar of Sexual Idolatry* (Dry Ridge, Kent.: Pure Life Ministries, 2000), 60.

Chapter 3: Meet Cain the Destroyer

1. Allen P. Ross, *Creation and Blessing* (Grand Rapids: Baker, 1988), 158.

2. Claus Westerman, as quoted in Ross, *Creation and Blessing,* 159.

Chapter 4: Families at War: When Trust Fails

1. *The Bible Knowledge Commentary,* ed. John F. Walvood and Roy B. Zuck (Wheaton, Ill.: Victor, 1983), 81.

Chapter 5: Dodging Spears

1. Gene Edwards, *A Tale of Three Kings* (Auburn, Me.: Christian Books, 1980), 40.

2. Ibid., 22.

Chapter 6: Christians in the Courtroom

1. Larry Burkett, "Opinion: Should Christians Sue?" www.pastors.com, 8 October

2003. Burkett's arguments were first presented in Larry Burkett, *Business by the Book* (Nashville: Nelson, 1990).

2. Ibid.

3. Three organizations that offer mediation or mediation referrals are Peacemaker Ministries (Billings Mont.), www.hispeace.org; the Christian Legal Society (Springfield, Va.), www.clsnet.com; and Metanoia Ministries (Washington, N.H.), www.changeyourmind.net.

Chapter 7: From Bitterness to Blessing

1. Source unknown.

Chapter 8: The High Cost of Reconciliation

1. This powerful story is detailed in Erwin Lutzer, *Flames of Freedom* (Chicago: Moody, 1976).

2. John Perkins, *Let Justice Roll Down* (Ventura, Calif.: Regal, 1976), 205.

3. Personal testimony given by Sammy Tippet, Colorado Springs, 22 August 2006.

Chapter 9: When Reconciliation Fails

1. R. T. Kendall, *Total Forgiveness* (Lake Mary, Fla.: Charisma, 2002), 33.

2. As quoted by Roma Wade in her "Red Book" collection on "Don Wade and Roma," WLS-AM radio, Chicago, 19 October 2004.

ISBN: 0-8024-6305-3
ISBN-13: 978-0-8024-6305-0

Death is not a hopeless plunge into the vast unknown.

Many people spend more time planning for a vacation than preparing for eternity. Perhaps it doesn't seem real that we will still exist—fully conscious and alive—beyond the grave. But it's true, and it calls for careful consideration. What can we expect one minute after we die? Be brave enough to find out.

by Erwin W. Lutzer
Find it now at your favorite local or online bookstore.
www.MoodyPublishers.com

How You Can Be Sure That You Will SPEND ETERNITY WITH God

Erwin W. Lutzer

ISBN: 0-8024-2719-7
ISBN-13: 978-0-8024-2719-9

In this concise and powerful book, Dr. Lutzer explains why you can know, even now, where you will be after death. He insists that many who expect to enter heaven will discover they are sadly mistaken. But it is not too late for those who are still living to choose the right path—and know it!

by Erwin W. Lutzer
Find it now at your favorite local or online bookstore.
www.MoodyPublishers.com